DIPLOMACY AND SECURITY IN THE SOUTH CHINA SEA: AFTER THE TRIBUNAL

HEARING

BEFORE THE

SUBCOMMITTEE ON ASIA AND THE PACIFIC

OF THE

COMMITTEE ON FOREIGN AFFAIRS
HOUSE OF REPRESENTATIVES

ONE HUNDRED FOURTEENTH CONGRESS

SECOND SESSION

SEPTEMBER 22, 2016

Serial No. 114–232

Printed for the use of the Committee on Foreign Affairs

Available via the World Wide Web: http://www.foreignaffairs.house.gov/ or
http://www.gpo.gov/fdsys/

U.S. GOVERNMENT PUBLISHING OFFICE

21–606PDF   WASHINGTON : 2016

For sale by the Superintendent of Documents, U.S. Government Publishing Office
Internet: bookstore.gpo.gov   Phone: toll free (866) 512–1800; DC area (202) 512–1800
Fax: (202) 512–2104   Mail: Stop IDCC, Washington, DC 20402–0001

COMMITTEE ON FOREIGN AFFAIRS

EDWARD R. ROYCE, California, *Chairman*

CHRISTOPHER H. SMITH, New Jersey
ILEANA ROS-LEHTINEN, Florida
DANA ROHRABACHER, California
STEVE CHABOT, Ohio
JOE WILSON, South Carolina
MICHAEL T. McCAUL, Texas
TED POE, Texas
MATT SALMON, Arizona
DARRELL E. ISSA, California
TOM MARINO, Pennsylvania
JEFF DUNCAN, South Carolina
MO BROOKS, Alabama
PAUL COOK, California
RANDY K. WEBER SR., Texas
SCOTT PERRY, Pennsylvania
RON DeSANTIS, Florida
MARK MEADOWS, North Carolina
TED S. YOHO, Florida
CURT CLAWSON, Florida
SCOTT DesJARLAIS, Tennessee
REID J. RIBBLE, Wisconsin
DAVID A. TROTT, Michigan
LEE M. ZELDIN, New York
DANIEL DONOVAN, New York

ELIOT L. ENGEL, New York
BRAD SHERMAN, California
GREGORY W. MEEKS, New York
ALBIO SIRES, New Jersey
GERALD E. CONNOLLY, Virginia
THEODORE E. DEUTCH, Florida
BRIAN HIGGINS, New York
KAREN BASS, California
WILLIAM KEATING, Massachusetts
DAVID CICILLINE, Rhode Island
ALAN GRAYSON, Florida
AMI BERA, California
ALAN S. LOWENTHAL, California
GRACE MENG, New York
LOIS FRANKEL, Florida
TULSI GABBARD, Hawaii
JOAQUIN CASTRO, Texas
ROBIN L. KELLY, Illinois
BRENDAN F. BOYLE, Pennsylvania

AMY PORTER, *Chief of Staff*   THOMAS SHEEHY, *Staff Director*
JASON STEINBAUM, *Democratic Staff Director*

———————

SUBCOMMITTEE ON ASIA AND THE PACIFIC

MATT SALMON, Arizona *Chairman*

DANA ROHRABACHER, California
STEVE CHABOT, Ohio
TOM MARINO, Pennsylvania
JEFF DUNCAN, South Carolina
MO BROOKS, Alabama
SCOTT PERRY, Pennsylvania
SCOTT DesJARLAIS, Tennessee

BRAD SHERMAN, California
AMI BERA, California
TULSI GABBARD, Hawaii
ALAN S. LOWENTHAL, California
GERALD E. CONNOLLY, Virginia
GRACE MENG, New York

CONTENTS

DIPLOMACY AND SECURITY IN THE SOUTH CHINA SEA: AFTER THE TRIBUNAL

THURSDAY, SEPTEMBER 22, 2016

HOUSE OF REPRESENTATIVES,
SUBCOMMITTEE ON ASIA AND THE PACIFIC,
COMMITTEE ON FOREIGN AFFAIRS,
Washington, DC.

The subcommittee met, pursuant to notice, at 2:00 p.m., in room 2172 Rayburn House Office Building, Hon. Matt Salmon (chairman of the subcommittee) presiding.

Mr. SALMON. Subcommittee will come to order. Members present will be permitted to submit written statements that will be included in the official record.

Without objection, the hearing record will remain open for 5 calendar days to allow statements, questions and extraneous materials for the record subject to the length limitation in the rules.

South China Sea is one of the toughest and most persistent problems in this subcommittee's jurisdiction. These maritime and territorial disputes are universally recognized as a long-term security challenge.

Mr. SHERMAN. Mr. Chairman? If I can just ask for permission to give my opening statement after the witnesses.

Mr. SALMON. Oh, I am sorry. Yes.

Mr. SHERMAN. Yes, I wanted to——

Mr. SALMON. Okay. Good.

Yes, Mr. Sherman will give his opening statement after the witnesses testify. He has actually got to go between a couple of different responsibilities today.

Back to what I was saying, the maritime and territorial disputes are universally recognized as a long-term security challenge and a potential short-term flashpoint.

Conflicting claims to the strategic waterways which connect maritime Asia endanger trade, transportation, commerce and energy flows, creating the risk of conflict.

China has taken the riskiest and most dangerous actions of any of any party to the disputes, seizing territory far from its shores, fielding huge fleets of Coast Guard and fishing vessels to bolster its claims and constructing military outposts throughout contested zones to consolidate its strategic position.

Despite the dire and worsening situation, recent developments have given the South China Sea an unfulfilled potential for positive progress.

This summer, an Arbital Tribune, constituted under the United Nations Convention on the Law of the Sea, issued an eagerly anticipated ruling in a case between China and the Philippines, bringing legal certainty to the obvious truth that China's claims on the South China Sea are illegitimate.

Though the international community cheered the ruling, its influence is still uncertain. Since the tribunal announced its ruling, the uncertain status quo has persisted in the South China Sea, and there have been signals that China plans to take its construction efforts to the Scarborough Shoal, a sensitive area right off the Philippines' shores, which would be a serious escalation.

At the same time, China has moved aggressively to generate diplomatic cover for its legally untenable and unjustifiable claims. Throughout the Association of Southeast Asian Nations (ASEAN) China has used surrogates to disrupt and block consensus, successfully preventing unified statements on the issue, at least in regional summits. There are also obvious signs of intense efforts to win more southeast Asian support for China's position.

For instance, Thailand recently stated its support for China's so-called efforts to maintain peace in the South China Sea, though Thailand is not a claimant to that dispute and has traditionally remained neutral on the issue.

Conduct from the Philippines during this period has been more and more disappointing. The Philippines' victory before the international tribunal was a shining example of the peaceful resolution of a dispute between two states based on legal principle as opposed to force.

It demonstrated the value of the system of international law that states have used cooperatively to avoid major conflict for decades.

Despite this victory, the Philippines has not leveraged the ruling in its dealings with China. The cool response was at first lauded as savvy diplomacy, but since then, things have become decidedly worse.

The new President, Rodrigo Duterte, has called into question the Philippines' dedication to the rule of law, creating a domestic crisis of widespread extrajudicial killing.

He's engaged in childish name calling toward President Obama and our Ambassador to the Philippines. He's announced his intention to end a longstanding and successful counter terror cooperation in Mindanao, raised the possibility of increasing arms acquisitions from China and Russia and spoken of ending joint maritime patrols with the U.S. Navy.

At the same time, the importance of the Philippines' legal victory has been downplayed or avoided altogether. President Duterte has affirmatively avoided the topic in his discussions with Chinese interlocutors, and he deliberately declined to raise the issue in a recent high-profile speech, throwing away his prepared remarks on the ruling at the last minute.

To be sure, many ASEAN states have good reason to evaluate critically their capacity and will to resist China's influence on the issue.

In virtually every case, modest defense capabilities and close economic ties mean that China is an undeniably important partner for each ASEAN country.

By playing their cards close to their chest while signaling potential compromise with China, southeast Asian nations seem to be navigating the post-ruling uncertainties of the South China Sea extremely cautiously, feeling out bilateral options and seeking the most advantageous near-term result at the cost of a collective response that might better suit each of their needs.

As in many other realms, responsibility falls to the United States in the South China Sea, not just to advance our allies' and partners' interests but to protect our own.

Every nation has a stake in the rule of law, the protection of territorial integrity and in peaceful dispute resolution.

In southeast Asia, where a vacuum of strategic military strength is being filled by China's rising forces, these interests are in jeopardy.

It falls to us to back stop our partners with our own strength and integrity and to remind those nations faltering under China's self-serving diplomatic assault what is at stake.

With our expert panel today, we will review the developments in the South China Sea disputes following the Arbital ruling with an eye toward formulating policy options to protect the freedom of navigation, the rule of law and peaceful dispute resolution.

We will also be looking to strengthen rather than weaken our relationships in the region in response to this challenge. And I look forward to the witnesses' recommendations for that as well. And, as we have mentioned earlier, the ranking member will make his opening statements after your comments.

And so I will start with the panel. Mr. Elbridge Colby, Senior Fellow at the Center for a New American Security; Dr. Dean Cheng, Senior Research Fellow at The Heritage Foundation's Asia Studies Center; Dr. Amy Searight, senior advisor and director of the Southeast Asia Program at CSIS; and Amitai Etzioni—did I say that right?

Mr. ETZIONI. Yes.

Mr. SALMON. Oh, good. Professor of international affairs at the George Washington University. We thank the panel for joining us today and for their expertise, and I will start with you, Mr. Colby.

STATEMENT OF MR. ELBRIDGE COLBY, ROBERT M. GATES SENIOR FELLOW, CENTER FOR A NEW AMERICAN SECURITY

Mr. COLBY. Mr. Chairman, Ranking Member Sherman and distinguished members of the committee, thank you very much for inviting me to testify today on the South China Sea.

It's an honor to speak with you on this matter of such importance to our Nation and to the Asia Pacific as a whole.

Put forthrightly, the United States should press back more firmly against China's assertiveness in the South China Sea both directly and indirectly, and Washington should be must less shy about doing so.

This course is likely to be more successful and stabilizing and, indeed, actually less risky than our current one, which is defined by a strange hesitancy on our part.

Right now, China appears to believe it can rock the boat and that we will take pains to right it. We seem to be more nervous about China's will and ability to escalate and the threat that such firmness would have on our broader relationship with Beijing than they are. This is strange, because despite what President Duterte says, we still hold many commanding advantages.

Our hesitancy seems to be leading Beijing to think it can continue pushing into the South China Sea and beyond. But, it is also leading regional states, both allies and partners as well as fence-sitters, to wonder whether it is prudent to work with us to balance and constrain China's assertiveness.

If Washington is so anxious and tepid when we are still so strong, what does that say about our willingness to act as China grows stronger in the coming years? It certainly cannot and does not inspire confidence.

Rectifying the situation requires resolute American leadership and sustained strength. Otherwise, states in the region are likely to be pulled toward accommodating rather than balancing Beijing.

Moreover, the situation today is more serious than is often admitted. The perception of American irresolution risks hardening into a judgment, and China's militarized islands in the Spratlys already pose more of a threat to U.S. forces and regional states than is commonly appreciated.

So what should we do? Our actions should be guided by two over-arching principles. First, we need to demonstrate greater resolve and willingness to bear and assume risk.

Second, we need to build up our allies' and partners' military and economic strength. In the first category, we should do the following.

Conduct more FONOPs and conduct them more assertively, while describing their purpose and justification more candidly and unabashedly.

At the same time, we should also conduct intense presence operations beyond those designed to vindicate U.S. legal positions. We should further encourage other like-minded countries like Japan, Australia, India and France, which has offered to coordinate EU patrols, to conduct their own FONOPs and/or presence operations either with us or separately.

Secondly, we should shrink the white hull loophole China is exploiting by making clear we will respond to coercion or aggression by such ''white hull ships'' with whatever means we deem appropriate, including military force.

China must not get a free pass by using technically nonmilitary ships for coercion or worse.

Third, we should deter Beijing's militarization of Scarborough Shoal by showing resolve, demonstrating our capability and studying the merits of extending the mutual defense treaty with Manila to the shoal.

Resolve is important, but military and economic power are even more so. China will only realistically be constrained if we are sufficiently strong. Accordingly, we need to strengthen our own hand and those of like mind. Thus, we should do the following.

First, increase and extend U.S. military advantages and presence in the region. This means prioritizing and maintaining our conventional advantage in the Western Pacific through efforts like the Third Offset and related initiatives.

Congress should fund and support these initiatives forward into the next administration. It also means increasing combat-credible

U.S. presence in the region including by continuing to shift forces and especially higher-end forces to the region.

Second, we should deepen military and other links with allies and partners and encourage their own indigenous efforts. This means expanding on the EDCA with Manila, despite the current turbulence in the relationship, capitalizing on Japan's interest in a broader footprint in the region and following through on openings to deepen engagement with states like India, Vietnam and Indonesia.

U.S. efforts should especially focus on building up like-minded states' ability to resist or complicate Chinese assertiveness, both at the gray zone level through assistance with maritime domain awareness and more patrol craft and the like, but also selectively at the higher end by helping to develop anti-access area denial capabilities of their own.

Third, and perhaps more importantly, we need to maintain U.S. economic leadership and leverage by ratifying TPP. A successful effort to balance China depends on a sense in the region of U.S. economic strength and leadership, especially in light of China's efforts to translate its own economic power into political leverage through efforts like the ''One Belt One Road'' initiative. TPP is crucial to such a successful effort.

Conversely, rejecting TPP would deal a blow, and perhaps a very formidable one, to the U.S. position in the region. The Congress should therefore provide its advice and consent to the pact's ratification as expeditiously as possible.

In sum, if the United States and other states fail to stop the expansion of China's power over the South China Sea, Beijing's ambitions are only likely to grow. If we succeed, however, a more stable and enduring balance is likely to result.

Accordingly, we must get the South China Sea right. I hope that the steps offered here would contribute to that goal. I look forward to any questions you might have.

Thank you very much.

[The prepared statement of Mr. Colby follows:]

Center for a
New American
Security

September 22, 2016

Testimony before the House Committee on Foreign Affairs Subcommittee on Asia and the Pacific "Diplomacy and Security in the South China Sea: After the Tribunal"

Elbridge A. Colby
Robert M. Gates Senior Fellow
Center for a New American Security

Mr. Chairman, Ranking Member Sherman, and distinguished members of the committee, thank you for inviting me to testify today on developments in and affecting the South China Sea and how the United States should respond to them. It is an honor to speak to you today on this matter of such importance to our nation and to the Asia-Pacific as a whole.

Put forthrightly, the United States should press back more firmly against China's assertiveness in the South China Sea, both directly and indirectly, and Washington should be much less shy about doing so. The reason is that the costs of continued tepidness are greater than often recognized, while the benefits of such caution are frequently exaggerated. Conversely, firmer action is likely to yield greater benefits and be less risky than is often supposed. This is because such greater firmness is more likely to change Beijing's calculus of how much it can push, and is therefore more likely to head off China's progressive expansion of its influence over an area of considerable significance for the United States. At the same time, it is also more likely to demonstrate to allies, partners, as well as fence-sitters in the region that aligning with the United States in working to restrain China's assertiveness is a reasonable and prudent thing to do.

Beijing's Ambitions in – and Beyond – the South China Sea

The core problem is well known: the effort by China, Asia's emerging behemoth, to establish an increasing degree of control and even dominance over a waterway of great strategic, economic, and geopolitical importance. It is true that the South China Sea is crisscrossed by a myriad of competing claims, that adjudicating the various claims is complex, and that the situation is fraught with the potential for miscalculation and escalation.

But these points should not obscure the heart of the matter. Beijing has set out tremendously expansive claims over the South China Sea in its "nine dash line"; forcefully advanced these claims through the use of quasi-military and military forces and an assertive and at times even aggressive diplomacy; built up and militarized features it has occupied; angrily denounced the Permanent Court of Arbitration ruling that essentially wholly dismissed its claims; and demonstrated the interest and the ability to continue pressing its claims and degree of control in the Sea. China has now established increasingly significant military footprints not only on Woody Island in the Paracels but also on Fiery Cross, Subi, and Mischief Reefs in the Spratly Islands much farther to the south; initiated civilian flights to its new manmade islands; and considerably upped its military and quasi-military presence in the area. Having established a formidable military footprint in the South China Sea, Beijing now appears to be reckoning how and when to take additional steps in its pursuit of sway over the area. Such steps could include, for instance, the imposition of an Air Defense Identification Zone (ADIZ) over the Sea or the militarization of Scarborough Shoal, which lies approximately 125 miles off the Philippine coast near Subic Bay. Indeed, news reports indicate that China may take advantage of U.S. inattention to foreign affairs during the general election campaign to make especially bold moves.[1]

If Beijing is left unchecked in effort to gain ascendancy over the region, U.S. interests will suffer, potentially very seriously. The South China Sea is a vital waterway that abuts most of the countries of Southeast Asia, and is the maritime thoroughfare through which an enormous amount of East Asia's commercial traffic flows. The state or states that can govern or dominate the Sea would therefore have tremendous leverage over those who border it or rely on the goods that pass through its waters. If China can achieve this kind of control – which appears to be its goal – it would be able to influence and coerce by economic means regional and other states reliant on transiting traffic and the Sea's development through its ability to regulate, interrupt, or facilitate commerce and economic activity in the area. Given the kinds of economic, political, and other arrangements China has been pushing in recent years, its revanchist and often domineering approach to international politics, and the nature of its political system, Beijing would be likely to use such economic leverage to push the regional economic and political order in directions unfriendly and possibly even inimical to U.S. interests and the kind of international system we have built and sustained since the Second World War. Nor would the impact of such influence and its use be confined to the region. The Western Pacific is increasingly the leading center of global economic activity, and thus its fate exercises an outsized impact on the broader world system.

But the implications of such dominance would not be confined to the economic domain. If China can secure suzerainty over the South China Sea, it could turn it into a "Chinese lake" and use its growing military strength – including its ability to project credible and effective military power – to overawe states in the region, including U.S. allies like the Philippines and Australia, partners like Singapore, and other states with which Washington has solid or improving relations like Vietnam, Indonesia, and Malaysia. At the same time, it could use its military strength to shadow or even threaten or block the vital commercial traffic that passes through the South China Sea to key U.S. allies like Japan and South Korea or to Taiwan. And, in the worst case event of conflict with the United States itself, Chinese control over the Sea would give Beijing a formidable position from which to attack, harass, and defend against U.S. and allied forces, and would make U.S. strategies designed to prevail over Beijing, for instance through a distant blockade, harder. It could also provide a secure bastion for Chinese ballistic missile submarines to safely operate and threaten U.S. targets, further darkening the shadow of China's nuclear deterrent over any potential conflict.

---

[1] Harry Kazianis, "Beijing may be waiting for the perfect timing to strike in South China Sea," *Asia Times*, September 15, 2016, http://atimes.com/2016/09/china-may-be-waiting-for-the-perfect-timing-to-strike-in-south-china-sea/.

It is therefore crucial for the United States, along with like-minded states, to prevent China from establishing control over the South China Sea. This is not only because ceding dominance there would significantly augment Beijing's ability to dictate the governance, the rules, and the nature of both international and domestic politics and economics in the region. Rather, China's ambitions in the South China Sea are very unlikely to end there, especially if they are easily realized. Instead, if Beijing can establish sway over the South China Sea, its ambitions are likely to expand farther outwards, into the broader Indo-Pacific and beyond. Indeed, it has been well noted that China's aspirations and interests have already expanded markedly in recent years.[2] This is not surprising – as countries' capabilities increase, so too are their ambitions likely to grow, just as individuals' wants and expectations are likely to expand as they grow wealthier and more powerful. China boasts, of course, a unique and distinctively great and proud culture, but Chinese state behavior is not immune from these normal tendencies of human beings and states. As anyone who has visited China can attest, contemporary Chinese society is not defined by a shy or retiring spirit. Rather, it is increasingly defined by what one of its most astute observers has called an "age of ambition," as a generation raised on 10% annual growth rates and a world acclaiming China's rise comes to eminence.[3] Why should we expect such a country to be abnormally restrained in its pursuit of what it deems its rightful place once it has the power to do so?

The Worsening Situation – and the Vital Role of the United States in Rectifying It

If China can establish dominance over the South China Sea, then, it would constitute a formidable blow to U.S. interests, a blow that we should very much strive to avoid. Fortunately, we are currently far from this dangerous eventuality – but not as comfortably far as many seem to think. This is primarily due to two factors. First, there is a fear that risks hardening into a conclusion in the region that the South China Sea is "going China's way" and that the United States is too reluctant or unwilling to take the actions needed to stem this trend. Second, China's militarization of the islands it occupies or has reclaimed and built up already pose a considerable military challenge.

Whether China will be able to establish dominance over the South China Sea is in large part a question of whether countries in the Indo-Pacific resolve to prevent it from happening. While China is very strong, it can be balanced and its behavior shaped by a coalition of countries in the region and the United States, primarily because these countries and especially the United States have and will have the power to balance a future PRC.[4] Power in the contemporary world is largely a function of economic vitality, and China is already experiencing very serious and potentially grave challenges to its growth model, challenges that will be very difficult for the Chinese government to address and resolve. China's growth rate has already slowed, and it is likely to come further down to earth, leading not only to more constraints on its rate of increase in expenditures on defense but also to

---

[2] Ely Ratner, Elbridge Colby, Andrew Erickson, Zachary Hosford, and Alexander Sullivan, "More Willing & Able: Charting China's International Security Activism" (Center for a New American Security, May 2015).

[3] Evan Osnos, *Age of Ambition: Chasing Fortune, Truth, and Faith in the New China* (New York: Farrar, Straus and Giroux, 2014).

[4] Ashley J. Tellis, "Balancing Without Containment: An American Strategy for Managing China" (Carnegie Endowment for International Peace, 2014).

internal tensions regarding how to manage the societal implications of this slowdown. At the same time, the U.S. economy remains a preferred destination for global capital and a rare outpost of relative growth in a slowing world economy. While the U.S. economy could certainly be doing much better and achieving such growth should catalyze substantial changes in U.S. domestic policies, U.S. long-term trends are relatively favorable.[5] What seems likely is that the long-term competition in power between the United States and China is likely to be that – a competition. It is therefore reasonable to judge that the United States will have the power, especially in concert with established economies like Japan and rising ones like India, to balance China.

But the role of the United States is and will be crucial in this effort. No country in the region wants to be left exposed as the balancer, alienating Beijing and triggering its ire in ways that can have very concrete consequences, as the Philippines and Japan have found out. Thus, even as many countries fear Chinese dominance, each country in the region has an incentive to be very cautious about provoking Beijing's wrath. This is the classic problem of collective action: coalitions do not just spontaneously come together; rather, they usually form because a particularly strong power leans forward and thereby demonstrates that it is reasonable and prudent to affiliate with it to balance the rising, worrying, or threatening state. The only country that can plausibly play this role is the United States. No coalition to balance China will form without the active leadership of Washington, a leadership that shows countries that have to live next door to China that coalescing to constrain it is a reasonable bet.

Yet the perspective in the region is that U.S. leadership on this front has sounded a very uncertain trumpet. The United States sometimes uses strong language to call out Chinese behavior, but sometimes does not, and occasionally even seems afraid or ashamed to be frank about what Beijing is doing. Reports in the press go so far as to indicate that Washington discourages, if it does not suppress, more candid statements from officials who are inclined to speak more frankly. More importantly, the United States has conducted some freedom of navigation operations (FONOPs), but fewer than might be expected, with less unabashed clarity about what they are doing and what their basis is, and with a more restricted purpose than our principles and interests would seem to dictate. Broadly, Washington seems highly concerned, and sometimes even fearful, about how Beijing will react to straightforward actions designed to demonstrate U.S. seriousness about its principles and its interests and those of its allies and partners. These fears seem to include anxieties about the potential for escalation in the region, deliberate and inadvertent, but also about how Beijing will respond with respect to the broader Sino-U.S. relationship on issues ranging from climate change to economic cooperation.

This evident anxiety does not appear to have been lost on Beijing, which seems to believe it can "rock the boat" in the South China Sea and that Washington will take pains to right it. As Washington appears more fearful of jeopardizing the broader relationship or of escalation than of failing to forcefully vindicate its interests and principles in the region, it is not particularly surprising that Beijing has continued its assertive policy. After all, it is paying dividends. Of course Beijing is

---

[5] Elbridge Colby and Paul Lettow, "Have We Hit Peak America? The Sources of U.S. Power and the Path to National Renaissance," *Foreign Policy*, July/August 2014, 54-63.

savvy enough to avoid directly confronting Washington, but "salami-slicing" tactics have already yielded China solid gains in the South China Sea and promise more unless countered.[6]

Moreover, if the situation seems too "hot" in the South China Sea, Beijing has evinced an ability to shift to pursuing its goals in the East China Sea, where Beijing lays claim to the Senkaku/Diaoyu Islands also claimed by Japan. In point of fact, China's activities have markedly increased in recent months in the East China Sea. After a period of relative quiet there, Chinese aircraft and ships, including some that appear to be armed, have substantially upped their presence and activities around the islands. In early August, about fifteen Chinese Coast Guard vessels, some of them apparently armed, escorted over 200 Chinese fishing vessels to the vicinity of the Senkakus, where some of these ships reportedly penetrated the nautical territorial limit.[7] This activity may have been aimed at deterring a more active Japanese presence in the South China Sea, particularly Tokyo's participation in FONOPs with Washington. Further such activities in the East China Sea seem likely.

Nor is Washington's reluctance noticed only in Beijing. Rather, it suggests to countries in the region currently reckoning how prudent it is to work with the United States to balance China that Washington is unwilling or believes it is or will be unable to stay in the region and lead an effort to restrain Beijing's assertiveness. Beijing's success in pressing its claims and the impunity with which it has done so, and the reluctance that Washington has exhibited in forcefully and concretely pushing back against these actions, in some ways has given China the political initiative and risks creating or confirming the perception that Chinese dominance of the area is inevitable. Earlier this month, new Philippine President Rodrigo Duterte bluntly expressed this sort of view: "China is now in power, and they have military superiority in the region," as he announced the end of joint naval patrols with the U.S. in the disputed South China Sea, and expelled U.S. forces from southern Mindanao.[8]

This is particularly disquieting because the United States, despite Duterte's comments, by almost all accounts still enjoys considerable advantage over Beijing in terms of national power, military and economic. So what does it suggest that Washington is as reluctant to press Beijing as it is today when it still enjoys a considerable margin of military and economic advantage? What does that portend for a future in which the power balance will be much more competitive? Concerns such as these make potential U.S. partners in the region open to more forthright and vigorous action or support much less keen to "stick their necks out." This is why statements from Administration representatives that China is alienating the region and thus acting in a self-defeating fashion are not persuasive. Without more emphatic policy and action by the United States, China's alienation of regional states may result more in intimidating and cowing rather than catalyzing them to press back against Beijing's actions.

---

[6] Elbridge Colby and Ely Ratner, "Roiling the Waters," *Foreign Policy*, January/February 2014, 10-13.

[7] Tim Kelly, "Japan says Chinese military activity in East China Sea escalating," *Reuters*, June 30, 2016, and Ankit Panda, "Japan: 7 Chinese Coast Guard Ships, 230 Fishing Boats in Disputed East China Sea Waters," *The Diplomat*, August 8, 2016.

[8] Bryan Harris and Michael Peel, "Philippines pivots away from the US," *Financial Times*, September 14, 2016.

The second reason that things are currently worse than many suppose is that China's militarization of its existing positions in the South China Sea and likely further efforts are considerably more significant than often admitted. This military progress is likely to give China added coercive leverage not only in the event of war but also in peacetime, as these forces not only constitute a considerable problem for U.S. forces but also represent a very serious potential threat to much-less capable regional states.

While there is much justified focus on the possibility for Beijing to militarize Scarborough Shoal, which would have major implications for the security of the Philippines, we should not forget that China has already occupied formations and established positions which few expect the Chinese to abandon. Fiery Cross, Subi, and Mischief Reefs are the most significant current Chinese bases. Each of these reefs is larger than often supposed; Subi is as wide as Pearl Harbor and Mischief as wide as the District of Columbia. Each is judged to boast 10,000 foot reinforced runways, deep water harbors, hardened hangars, impressive support facilities, housing for personnel, and the potential to host additional forces, personnel, and facilities. These reefs – now really manmade islands – could each house a fighter regiment; surface-to-air, anti-ship, and surface-to-surface missiles; intelligence, surveillance, and reconnaissance assets such as radars and other sensors; and other military capabilities. China has already apparently deployed sophisticated surface-to-air missile batteries to Woody Island in the Paracels; there is no technical block to it deploying such or similar advanced systems to its reclaimed islands deeper south and east into the Sea.[9]

While it is true that U.S. forces could destroy or degrade these types of forces and facilities in the event of a conflict, it is also true that such forces could give China important military advantages in the event of such a war by providing significant strike and defensive capabilities against U.S. and allied forces and logistics chains in the air and space domains, at and under the sea, and on land in surrounding areas, ultimately forcing U.S. forces to have to fight in from farther out, and do so with considerably greater difficulty. Destroying such Chinese fortifications would certainly be feasible for U.S. forces, but it is unlikely to be as easy or as cheap as many seem to believe.[10]

Moreover, such facilities and capabilities do not only affect the United States. Rather, these bases will provide Beijing with significantly added and more prompt military capability against regional states, which lack the U.S. ability to penetrate Chinese anti-access/area denial umbrellas and conduct effective sophisticated precision strike campaigns. They will therefore cast a darker shadow of Chinese coercive leverage over states in the region.

The Outlines of a More Effective South China Sea Policy

Thus the situation in the South China Sea is serious, and increasingly so. What, then, should the United States do?[11] U.S. actions should be guided by two overarching principles: first, in the nearer-

[9] I am grateful to Commander Thomas Shugart, USN, for much of this information, which is based on a working paper of his.

[10] Elbridge Colby and Evan Montgomery, "Changing Tides in the South China Sea," *The Wall Street Journal*, August 26, 2015.

[11] For a view of this question in a broader context, see Patrick M. Cronin, "Power and Order in the South China Sea: A Strategic Framework for U.S. Policy" (Center for a New American Security, 2016

term, to demonstrate greater resolve and willingness to risk escalation or the broader relationship with China, both to show to Beijing the perils of further assertiveness and to make clear to regional states that affiliating with the United States in such an effort is a safe course; and, second, to build up U.S. and allied military and economic strength to give Washington and its confederates as powerful a position as possible for the longer-term competition with China.

Demonstrating U.S. Resolve More Forcefully and Clearly in the Face of Chinese Assertiveness

Key policy initiatives to demonstrate U.S. resolve in the South China Sea include:

- **FONOPs and presence operations**
- **Shrinking the white hull loophole**
- **Deterring Chinese militarization of Scarborough Shoal**

FONOPs and Presence Operations: For the near-term, the United States should strive to rectify the perception that it is too timid about pushing back against Beijing's assertions in the South China. At a minimum, this entails conducting more FONOPs, conducting them more clearly to challenge Chinese legal claims, and doing so with a more forthright and unabashed explanation of what the United States is doing and why. In addition to FONOPs, the United States should also conduct intense presence operations beyond those designed to vindicate U.S. legal positions in order to demonstrate U.S. interest, resolve, and ability to maintain its position in the region. At a minimum, the United States should maintain a DDG in the area and as frequently as tenable bring CVNs and associated naval vessels and air wings into the region as well.

At the same time, the United States should also encourage other states – both in the Asia-Pacific and beyond – to conduct FONOPs as well as other presence activities with the United States singly or with other like-minded countries designed to challenge or more indirectly undermine Beijing's expansive claims. Japan and Australia, for instance, have been commendably active in this respect both in the air and at sea, with Tokyo just recently announcing its willingness to conduct joint operations with the United States in the South China Sea (although its willingness to conduct FONOPs is less clear, and may be the object of Chinese coercive manipulation in the East China Sea).[12] India has also indicated an openness to lending its involvement to some types of such activities. But the United States should not only look to states in the region. France, for instance, has taken a leading role in making clear its willingness to conduct patrols in the South China Sea in order to show its support for international law and freedom of navigation. Paris has further laudably expressed its willingness to coordinate additional European patrols in the South China Sea.[13] The United States should actively pick up and encourage opportunities along these lines to demonstrate

---

[forthcoming]).

[12] I am grateful to Matthew Pottinger for this observation.

[13] Jean-Yves Le Drian, "The Challenges of Conflict Resolution" (Speech at the IISS Shangri-La Dialogue, Singapore, June 3, 2016), and Yo-Jung Chen, "South China Sea: The French Are Coming," *The Diplomat*, July 14, 2016.

that Chinese assertiveness in the South China Sea will not be met with quiescence but rather with – at a minimum – a significant international political cost.

Shrinking the White Hull Loophole: China has for several years exploited its advantages in the number and sophistication of its so-called "white-hulled" non-military but large and capable vessels – for instance operated by the Chinese Coast Guard and fisheries administration – to pursue its claims, demonstrate presence, and at times to take aggressive action against rival claimants. The classification of these ships as "non-military" and the acceptance of this categorization by other states has allowed China to minimize the risk of counter-escalation by the United States and others while enabling it to pursue very assertive tactics. Accordingly the United States should seek to blur the distinction between white and "gray-hulled" (or military) vessels by stating that it will respond to physical assault or coercion by any ship with the means it deems appropriate, including military means if necessary. China must not get a free pass by using technically non-military ships.

Deterring Chinese Militarization of Scarborough Shoal: China's activities around the Scarborough Shoal have increased markedly in the last months. Recent reports indicate that Beijing may be considering militarizing the feature along the lines of what it has done in the Spratlys. Such an action would give China a highly valuable military outpost that could cover most of Luzon with surface-to-air missile and strike systems, and that lies just outside the major Philippine (and former American) naval base at Subic Bay. Scarborough's militarization would therefore represent a significant threat to the security and integrity of the Philippines and to U.S. forces there. Fears that Beijing might take this step have been substantial enough to have led Washington at the highest levels to communicate to Beijing the gravity with which the United States would regard such a step and to the deployment of the USS *John Stennis* to buttress that message.[14] Washington should continue sending such messages to ensure Beijing does not militarize Scarborough Shoal, and take additional steps such as conducting FONOPs and active presence operations as well as by encouraging international efforts to condemn any such act.

Washington should also consider the merits of formally extending the Mutual Defense Treaty with the Philippines to Scarborough, a step it has not yet taken, in part due to the legal uncertainty surrounding the competing claims. This would undoubtedly provoke Beijing and would expand Washington's commitment to the Philippines just as Manila under the Duterte Administration risks undermining warming U.S.-Philippine ties. Accordingly, such a step should not be taken lightly or inadvisedly, or without Philippine support and interest. Nonetheless, if the implications of China's militarization of the Shoal are as deleterious as some have suggested, it may well behoove the United States to formally include it in the ambit of the Treaty, especially given the clarity of the U.S. commitment to the Philippines and the increasing U.S. military presence there.[15]

---

[14] Michael McDevitt, "Is it Time for the U.S. to Take a Position on Scarborough Shoal?" *USNI News*, July 19, 2016.

[15] Dan de Luce, "At Scarborough Shoal, China Is Playing With Fire: Retired Admiral," *Foreign Policy*, June 16, 2016, and Matthew Pennington, "ADM Dennis Blair: U.S. Should Protect Philippine's Scarborough Shoal," Associated Press, July 15, 2016.

Beyond Demonstrations of Resolve: Increasing U.S. and Allied Military and Economic Power and Leverage

While these demonstrations of resolve to vindicate our interests and assert our legal positions are important, they are not enough. They do not increase our strength or that of those who share our interest in constraining China's assertiveness. And ultimately the fate of the South China Sea will be highly influenced by the relative strength – especially the military and economic strength – of the states involved, including the United States. The United States must therefore do more than simply show resolve. Rather, it must build up its own capabilities as well as those of its allies, partners, and those who share our common goal. This will provided added leverage and deterrent power, which will be more likely to dissuade China and place less weight on our resolve, which is important especially given the manifold interests Washington has around the world.

Accordingly, the United States should work to:

- **Increase and extend U.S. military advantages and presence in the region**
- **Deepen alliances and partnerships, and encourage allied and partner efforts and initiative**
- **Maintain U.S. economic leadership by ratifying TPP**

Increase and Extend U.S. Military Advantages and Presence in the Region: Elemental to a successful U.S. strategy in the region is sustained U.S. military superiority in maritime Asia. Without that military advantage, Beijing could plausibly win a war against the United States in the region. If China gains the military edge, Beijing's incentives to push forward will dramatically grow and third countries' incentives to affiliate or work with Washington to constrain Beijing will dramatically decrease. While U.S. military superiority certainly cannot handle all problems generated by China's assertiveness, particularly challenges in the "gray zone," in its absence these challenges would become much more severe and difficult to handle. Indeed, should China be able to attain military superiority in the Western Pacific, U.S. options might be reduced to relying more on its or others' nuclear deterrent or to abandoning its position. Needless to say, this is an eventuality the United States should very much want to avoid – as, it should be clearly and plainly emphasized to Beijing, should China.[16]

Accordingly, the United States must prioritize sustaining its military advantages with respect to maritime Asia (which, it should be noted, will generally also be applicable to contingencies involving Russia). This means vigorously implementing, resourcing, and extending into the next administration the Pentagon's "Third Offset Strategy" and related initiatives, initiatives designed to leverage U.S. advantages in technology, innovation, and organizational and cultural adaptiveness to extend U.S. conventional superiority. It also means adequately funding and supporting the development of capabilities suited to deterring China, for instance by developing and procuring new and sufficient numbers of attack submarines and penetrating strike platforms like the B-21 and associated weaponry, novel technologies such as unmanned and autonomous systems, a more resilient and

---

[16] Elbridge Colby, "Asia Goes Nuclear," *The National Interest* (January/February 2015), 28-37.

formidable space architecture, and the nuclear Triad and associated systems.[17] This necessitates lifting the sequester caps and providing the Department of Defense with adequate funding to meet its increasingly pressing requirements as well as the spending and management flexibility needed to optimize its expenditures and efforts.[18]

Presence is also important. It is not lost on regional countries that, while the United States may currently enjoy advantages at the level of large-scale, high-end conventional warfare, U.S. forces in the region are smaller in number and more rarely seen, while China's increasingly capable forces are present and prepared to butt heads with rival claimants, as Vietnam discovered in its 2014 altercation with Chinese vessels over the placement by Beijing of an oil rig in disputed waters. The United States should therefore continue shifting forces, especially high-end forces, more to the Asia-Pacific, but also look for innovative and creative ways to increase presence operations in the Western Pacific and the South China Sea in particular. This could include homeporting an additional U.S. aircraft carrier as well as associated carrier air wings in Japan, moving more SSNs to Guam, undertaking further Air Force and Navy rotations to Australia and the Philippines, and conducting more port visits and rotational ship deployments to Vietnam. The United States should also ensure its forward presence capabilities are combat-credible, since a force that is prepared to fight and prevail is more likely to achieve the deterrent purposes of forward presence than one that is vulnerable and largely symbolic.[19]

Deepen Alliances and Partnerships, and Encourage Allied and Partner Efforts and Initiative: A particularly vital step is to capitalize on opportunities to deepen military and other security links with existing allies and partners, and to expand such relationships with others in the region of like mind about the challenge from China, such as Vietnam and potentially Indonesia. This will not only enable the United States to better work with these states but also encourage them in their efforts to help balance China and help give them the means to do so.

This means following through and expanding on the Enhanced Defense Cooperation Agreement (EDCA) with the Philippines, despite the current political turbulence in our relations with Manila; on opportunities for rotational deployments and broader access arrangements with Australia; and on increasing interest in and capability for presence and operations in the region on the part of Japan. It also means the United States should look for opportunities to deepen engagement with Vietnam and with India; in both of these militarily significant countries there is a substantial sense of the value of deepening security relations with Washington in order to help balance China's growing power. The United States should also explore opportunities to work with countries like Indonesia that have expressed concern about Beijing's behavior and intentions but have been less active in their

---

[17] Robert O. Work, "The Third U.S. Offset Strategy and its Implications for Partners and Allies" (Speech at the ACT-CNAS Transatlantic Forum, Washington, D.C., January 28, 2015); and Shawn Brimley, "Arresting the Erosion of America's Military Edge," Statement to the Armed Services Committee, U.S. Senate, October 29, 2015.

[18] See, for instance, William J. Perry, John P. Abizaid, et al, *Ensuring a Strong U.S. Defense for the Future: The National Defense Panel Review of the 2014 Quadrennial Defense Review* (United States Institute of Peace, July 2014).

[19] Elbridge Colby and Jonathan F. Solomon, "Avoiding Becoming a Paper Tiger: Presence in a Warfighting Defense Strategy," *Joint Force Quarterly*, 82 no. 3 (July 2016), 24-32.

response. It also means encouraging deeper cooperation among these states, rather than insisting that all roads lead through Washington.

U.S. efforts should particularly focus on building up regional state capacity to resist or complicate Chinese assertiveness. The Maritime Security Initiative offers a commendable example of this type of initiative. U.S. focus should concentrate on helping regional states deal with Chinese gray zone challenges through better maritime and aerial domain awareness, such as a common operating picture in the South China Sea, and more and better vessels and aircraft to respond to such activities.[20] The United States should be able to sell more patrol boats, for instance, to the Philippines and Vietnam, and should pursue the concept of establishing a region-wide training center for such activities, potentially on Guam. But U.S. efforts should also selectively include sales or transfers of or support for acquisition of higher-end military capabilities that can help capable allies, partners, and other regional states build up anti-access and area denial capabilities of their own against Chinese higher-end forces, such as those operating from Beijing's new facilities in the South China Sea.

Washington should also encourage efforts by countries such as Japan in their own initiatives to build friendly state capacity and capability. This is especially significant given the liberalization of Tokyo's defense export restrictions.

Maintain U.S. Economic Leadership by Ratifying TPP: The success of any U.S. strategy in the Asia-Pacific cannot and will not, however, derive only from diplomacy and military means. Rather, economic steps are likely to be as, if not more, important, given Asia's level of development and the region's broadly shared view of the centrality of economics. Fortunately, the United States still enjoys a great deal of respect, leverage, and attraction in Asia as a trading partner, destination for and source of capital, example of successful business and innovation, and the like.

But China has sharply eroded that traditional advantage through its own growth and development as well as through conscious policies designed to create and enable the exercise of economic power for political or strategic ends, such as the "One Belt One Road" initiative. This power is not at all lost on regional states, many of which are fearful of Chinese ambitions and strength but also do not want to lose out on the chance to share in China's growing wealth and investment. This is true not only in places like Indonesia and Malaysia but also within established U.S. allies like Australia and the Philippines. Indeed, any coalition designed to constrain China, however loose, is likely to involve states – including the United States – sensibly seeking to balance that objective against the desire or need for positive commercial relations with China. We no longer live in the highly bifurcated, segregated world of the Cold War or the interwar period, in which rivals had little commerce or interaction with one another. Rather, contemporary international politics is likely to resemble traditional international politics, in which rivalry and competition coexisted with substantial commercial and other intercourse.

---

[20] Van Jackson, Mira Rapp-Hooper, Paul Scharre, Harry Krejsa, and Jeff Chism, "Networked Transparency: Constructing a Common Operational Picture of the South China Sea" (Center for a New American Security, March 2016).

Crucial in this world, therefore, is for the United States to have as much economic influence, credibility, and leverage of its own in the Asia-Pacific as possible. The Trans-Pacific Partnership Agreement (TPP) is the cornerstone of this effort. TPP has been exhaustively negotiated among twelve countries and the terms of the pact appear, according to the bulk of respected authorities on this subject, to be net beneficial for the U.S. economy.[21] But its strategic impact is clear. Although TPP is obviously a consensus document, it is also a product of American leadership, and reflects our established approach to markets and international trade, including in ways that demand sacrifices from other signatories as well as ourselves. Its ratification by the United States would signal the continued commitment of the United States to deep engagement with the Asia-Pacific. Moreover, it would create a large and powerful bloc of trading countries whose influence and common commitment to the pact would promote the adoption of its rules, standards, and values among those interested in becoming a part of it or of conducting commerce with its members.

Conversely, rejecting TPP would deal a blow, perhaps a very formidable one, to the U.S. position in the region, as friendly leaders such as Prime Minsters Abe of Japan and Lee of Singapore have emphasized. The United States would thereby abdicate any pretense to leadership in the region on trade and setting the rules and norms of economic engagement, potentially ceding that role to China. Moreover, it would signal that the United States might well not be as deeply and enduringly committed to its role in Asia as Washington has proclaimed so consistently, giving greater weight to incentives for regional states to accommodate China and its assertive approach.[22]

The Congress should therefore provide its advice and consent to the ratification of TPP as expeditiously as possible.

Conclusion

We live in a time in which many Americans are vigorously questioning the value of maintaining our post-war strategy of deep engagement abroad. This is not in and of itself unjustified or unfounded. Indeed, it is vital that U.S. foreign policy serve the interests of the American people, and that that connection be explained, not just assumed. Foreign policy is not missionary work, in the old phrase, and many things that happen abroad do not justify or require the commitment of U.S. forces, credibility, or money.

But such deep and sustained engagement, albeit of a more focused and balanced sort, remains worthwhile and indeed crucial.[23] If the United States withdraws from its key commitments in the most important regions of the globe, it is very likely to find that the world and the international order that results far less friendly and quite possibly more hostile and chaotic than if we had stayed

---

[21] Greg Mankiw, "An Open Letter," Greg Mankiw's Blog at gregmankiw.blogspot.com, March 5, 2015, http://gregmankiw.blogspot.com/2015/03/an-open-letter.html.

[22] See, for instance, the speech of Prime Minister Abe to a joint session of Congress on April 29, 2015, and the remarks of Singapore Prime Minister Lee Hsien Long available at http://warontherocks.com/2016/08/this-asian-leader-just-made-the-best-case-for-tpp-and-americas-role-in-asia/.

[23] Elbridge Colby and Jim Thomas, "The Future of Alliance," *The National Interest* (July/August 2016), 32-40.

involved. Moreover, we are quite likely to be pulled back into involvement even if we try to extricate ourselves, but with our credibility dashed and our ties dramatically weakened. Accordingly, an intelligent and sustainable strategy of engagement remains the best long-term course for our country; it is the strategy of "enlightened self-interest": long-term gains resulting from short-term sacrifices and risks.

This does not mean things should not change. Rather, in a more competitive and contested international political environment, we must be more selective and focused in how we spend our political and economic capital, and in how our nation elects to employ military force. Moreover, we must insist on greater assistance and burden-sharing from our allies and partners. But this also means we must show strength, resolve, and staying power in the face of rising powers that are increasingly interested in challenging us, our allies and partners, and the system we have jointly constructed and maintained.

In such a world, we must, however, prioritize. The United States faces manifold threats and challenges, but not all are of equal moment. China is the only country or force that has the power and potentially the will to upend the established order in the world's wealthiest region and perhaps globally, and the only one that could plausibly generate the military power to project significant armed might beyond its immediate environs and the economic power to cow or coerce major states. It is therefore crucial that the United States and other like-minded states ensure that China sees that restraint and respect for our interests and for established, albeit updated, norms and rules is the more prudent course. The only way to do that is through a consistent, long-term policy that balances engagement and cooperation with firmness, strength, and deterrence.

The South China Sea is and will be a central part of all of this. If the United States and other states fail to stop the expansion of China's power over such an important area, Beijing's strength and ambitions are only likely to grow. Conversely, if the United States and its partners succeed in constraining such expansion, then it is far more likely that a stable and enduring balance is likely to result. Accordingly, the United States must get the South China Sea right. The steps offered here should help to achieve this.

Mr. SALMON. Thank you.

Mr. Cheng.

STATEMENT OF MR. DEAN CHENG, SENIOR RESEARCH FELLOW, ASIAN STUDIES CENTER, THE HERITAGE FOUNDATION

Mr. CHENG. Chairman Salmon, Ranking Member Sherman, distinguished members of the committee, my name is Dean Cheng. I'm the senior research fellow for Chinese political and security affairs at The Heritage Foundation.

I would like to begin by expressing my appreciation for the opportunity to be here this afternoon and to note that the views I express are my own and should not be construed as representing any official position of The Heritage Foundation.

My comments today will focus on the military and security side of the growing Chinese challenge to Asian maritime security.

The past quarter century has seen a substantial improvement in the capabilities of the Chinese People's Liberation Army, or PLA.

With the PLA Navy we have seen the introduction of several new classes of surface combatants. The newest Chinese destroyer, the Type 052D, is comparable to our own Arleigh Burke DDG-51 Class.

The Chinese Type 054A frigate is both more capable and, let me note here, more reliable than our Littoral Combat Ship, both types of which are now sidelined due to engineering problems.

We know the Chinese are producing multiple classes of submarines and at least one new aircraft carrier is under construction.

China's naval combatants are among the youngest in average age, thanks to this major shipbuilding program. As important, China is not neglecting the key issue of maritime support.

China is building a fleet train of logistic support ships which will allow the Chinese navy to operate for extended periods away from shore.

Chinese submarines operating in the Indian Ocean have been accompanied by submarine tenders, allowing them to operate for longer periods away from Chinese ports.

China, of course, has now also begun construction on a new facility in Djibouti, their first formal overseas military base, but probably not their last.

Given the importance of air power for the Asia Pacific region, it is worth noting how the PLA Air Force, or PLAAF, is working on both the J-20 and J-31 fifth generation fighters.

China is the only other nation to be fielding two stealth fighter programs at the same time. Chinese bombers are now overflying islands in the South China Sea, and as these aircraft can be equipped with long-range anti-ship and land attack cruise missiles, the signal being sent to China's neighbors are very clear.

Again, the Chinese are also not neglecting the haft of the spear even as they sharpen the tip. China has introduced air transports to allow power projection and electronic warfare aircraft and AWACS to allow them the same kinds of advantages that our Air Force enjoys.

Most worrisome is the new PLA Strategic Support Force, which brings together under one service space warfare, electronic warfare and network warfare capabilities, reflecting the ongoing Chinese effort to establish information dominance, which the Chinese see as the central key to winning future what they term local wars under informationized conditions.

The objection of all of these various force improvements at the military level is to support China's move from a near-shore strategy of the 1960s to the near-sea strategy of the 1990s to today's far-seas approach, pushing Chinese military capability ever more extended distances from China's shores and deeper into the central Pacific and the Indian Ocean.

The shift reflects not only Chinese growing capabilities, but a broader transition in Chinese strategic thinking, which affects not only the military but national security thinking as a whole.

For the military, the extending reach is part of China's new historic missions, and while we must never forget that the People's Liberation Army is a party army where every officer is a member of the Chinese Communist Party, it nonetheless has also been charged with the responsibility of defending party and also national interests. Those national interests now include the seas, outer space and the electromagnetic spectrum.

China increasingly sees its fundamental security as tied to the world's oceans. This should not be surprising. China's economic center of gravity is now on its shores.

There is no longer a buffer of millions of square miles of territory between the Chinese economic center and the ocean's from which American and other allied capabilities spring.

At the same time, China itself is also more dependent on the sea for access to resources of power—Chinese economic growth. China is now a net importer of not only oil but food, including wheat, barley, sorghum and even rice.

Indeed, China is unique in being a traditional continental power that has become dependent on the seas. Napoleonic France, Wilhelmine Germany, the Soviet Union—all of these were continental powers for whom navies were luxuries or added benefits.

For China, it has become a central part of their economic existence. Unfortunately, as a result, the Chinese effort to safeguard its interests is expressed by extending Chinese sovereignty over what had been international common spaces. China's efforts to bring the South China Sea into the umbrella of Chinese control has led to remarkably intemperate remarks regarding the Permanent Court of Arbitration's findings.

The Chinese foreign minister termed them, ''a political farce.'' The Ambassador to the United States termed them, ''a matter of professional incompetence.''

What this suggests, and what this should serve as a warning, is that the United States, as the keystone upholding international order and the main advocate for international law and norms, must respond strongly through a combination of FONOPs, arms sales, robust presence but, above all, countering Chinese efforts at political warfare to undermine the legitimacy of the international order.

Thank you very much.

[The prepared statement of Mr. Cheng follows:]

The
Heritage Foundation

CONGRESSIONAL TESTIMONY

China and Asian Maritime Security
Testimony before the Subcommittee on Asia and the Pacific
Committee on Foreign Affairs

U.S. House of Representatives

September 22, 2016

Dean Cheng
Senior Research Fellow, Asian Studies Center
The Heritage Foundation

Chairman Royce, Representative Engel, and Members of the House Foreign Affairs Committee. Thank you for the opportunity to testify to you this morning.

My name is Dean Cheng, and I am a Senior Research Fellow in the Asian Studies Center of the Kathryn and Shelby Cullom Davis Institute for National Security and Foreign Policy at The Heritage Foundation. The views I express in this testimony are my own and should not be construed as representing any official position of The Heritage Foundation.

The rise of Chinese maritime capabilities makes it the first new maritime power to take to the seas since the end of the 19th century. Unlike Wilhelmine Germany or the Soviet Union, both of which fielded substantial navies, the People's Republic of China (PRC) actually relies upon the oceans for much of its economic activity. This dependence upon the sea also constitutes a radical break from that country's millennia of history; the imperial treasure fleets of Admiral Zheng He were not nearly as central to Chinese power and livelihood. Thus, the transformation of the PRC from a land power to a maritime one constitutes one of the more fundamental changes in the international scene, certainly since the end of the Cold War, and arguably over the past century.

Consequently, it has distinct implications for the security of the United States, and the Asian region.

China—Traditionally a Continental Power

For most of China's history, it was a continental power, focused on threats and opportunities on land. Compared to the Hsiung-Nu and the Mongols, the threats from the sea were minimal. As important, imperial China never depended upon the seas for its economic livelihood. While coastal traffic was used to move foodstuffs, the bulk of China's trade and economic activity was centered on land.

Imperial China did not wholly ignore the sea. As early as the 10th century AD, China had already developed the technology to build dry docks, facilitating the construction and repair of larger ships. Europe did not develop this same technology until the 15th century.[1] Similarly, the ships of Admiral Zheng He's treasure fleets, which sailed as far as the African coast in the early 15th Century, included such technology as watertight bulkheads. These ships, moreover, may have been as large as three times the size of HMS *Victory*, Nelson's flagship at Trafalgar.[2]

The fate of Zheng He's treasure ships and China's shipbuilding capabilities after his voyages, however, provide a cautionary tale for Chinese planners today. After his last voyage in 1433, Chinese officials lost interest in the seas. Construction of new ocean-going ships were banned, the shipyards that built them were shut down. Ocean-going trade was discouraged.

The consequences of this abandonment of the sea were displayed in the course of the First Sino–Japanese War (or the Jiawu War) of 1894–1895. Despite fielding technologically capable ships, the Chinese Beiyang Fleet was thoroughly defeated by the Imperial Japanese Navy, and the Qing Dynasty was forced to cede Taiwan to the Japanese empire, as well as relinquish influence over Korea.

Modern Chinese scholars and analysts view this history as a cautionary tale for today's government.

China Increasingly Depends on the Sea

For today's Chinese leadership, the ability to access and exploit the sea is essential. Since the rise of Deng Xiaoping in the early 1980s, China has become far more dependent upon the world's oceans, in large part because it has become thoroughly integrated into the global economy.

In 2014, the top sources of imports for China, i.e., where items are being sent to China, include:[3]

Nation	Percent	Value (Billions)
Republic of Korea	9.3%	$142
U.S.	8.8%	$134
Japan	8.5%	$131
Germany	6.3%	$96.7

The vast bulk of these imports are delivered by sea.

Similarly, China is increasingly dependent upon imported energy to keep its cities lit and its factories running. In 2014, the PRC became the world's largest net importer of petroleum, bringing in some 6.1 million barrels per day.[4] In 2016, despite a slowing economy, Chinese oil imports reached 8 million barrels per day.[5] While some is shipped via rail and pipelines, most is transported by sea.

China is also now a net importer of key agricultural products. This includes grain, soybeans and oilseeds, and fats and oils. Although China produces most of its own meat and dairy products, the U.S. Department of Agriculture notes that there is an increasing reliance on imports in this sector as well.[6]

This growing dependence on the sea to operate various parts of its economy and maintain its society makes China unique. China is arguably the first continental power that is truly dependent upon the sea. Unlike Napoleonic France, Wilhelmine Germany, or the Soviet Union, China cannot look upon the sea as an optional area of operation, but as a vital area of national interest.

Chinese National Security Is Increasingly Tied to the Sea

This growing dependence on the sea makes maritime concerns an essential part of Chinese national security calculations. This is exacerbated by China's increased vulnerability to seaborne threats. Under Mao Zedong, the Chinese leadership poured billions of dollars into developing the "third front" of defense industries, locating military industries deep in the Chinese interior (e.g., Shaanxi, Ningxia, and Sichuan Provinces). The goal was to provide millions of square miles of territory (and potential defenses) to shield them from possible attack from either the United States or the Soviet Union.[7]

By contrast, since the rise of Deng Xiaoping in the 1980s and the diversification of China's manufacturing base, China's economic center of gravity has shifted toward the the coast. This has allowed such economic centers as Shenzhen, Shanghai, and Pudong to more easily access global trade routes for both imports of raw materials and exports of products. This has meant, however, that China's recent economic development is also more vulnerable to potential attack from the sea.

Chinese leaders have therefore made clear that maritime concerns are increasingly part of China's fundamental interests. State Councilor Dai Bingguo, in 2009, stated that China would maintain

1. Louise Levathes, *When China Ruled the Seas* (NY: Oxford University Press, 1994), p. 77.
2. Edward Dreyer, *Zheng He* (NY: Pearson Publishing, 2007), pp. 106 and 113.
3. Figures from The Observatory of Economic Complexity, "China," http://atlas.media.mit.edu/en/profile/country/chn/ (accessed September 19, 2016).
4. US Energy Information Administration, "China," May 14, 2015, http://www.eia.gov/beta/international/analysis_includes/countries_long/China/china.pdf (accessed September 19, 2016).
5. Jenny W. Hsu, "Despite Slowdown, China's Oil Imports Surge," Marketwatch, March 7, 2016, http://www.marketwatch.com/story/despite-slowdown-chinas-oil-imports-surge-2016-03-07 (accessed September 19, 2016).
6. Fred Gale, James Hansen, and Michael Jewison, "China's Growing Demand for Agricultural Imports," U.S. Department of Agriculture, *Economic Information Bulletin* No. 136, February 2015, p. 4, http://www.ers.usda.gov/media/1784488/eib136.pdf (accessed September 19, 2016).
7. Barry Naughton, "The Third Front: Defence Industrialization in Chinese Interior," *The China Quarterly*, Vol. 115 (September 1988).

our core interests. And for China, our concern is we must uphold our basic systems, our national security; and secondly, the sovereignty and territorial integrity; and thirdly, economic and social sustained development.[8]

Those core interests include maritime concerns; sovereignty and territorial integrity pertains not only to land features but maritime ones as well. Indeed, the Chinese have termed their maritime claims as "blue soil," underscoring their importance.[9]

Some Chinese officials have gone even further. When the Chinese state-owned oil company China National Offshore Oil Company (CNOOC) launched the deep-sea drilling platform Haiyang Shiyou 981, the company's chairman declared that "large deepwater drilling rigs are our mobile national territory."[10] It is difficult to imagine risking such an expensive asset by a state-owned company without approval from higher political authorities. Yet, in May 2014, CNOOC deployed Haiyang 981 into disputed waters off Vietnam, initiating nearly two months of increased tension.

Xi Jinping himself has linked maritime interests and core interests. In July 2013, Xi stated to a Politburo study session that while China would pursue the path of peaceful development, it would "never abandon its legitimate maritime rights and interests, and furthermore, it will never sacrifice its core national interests."[11] The importance of the maritime domain to Chinese national security was further emphasized when it was included in the 2015 National Security Law. Article 17 of the law states that China will increase

the construction of border defense, coastal defense, and air defense, taking all necessary defense and control measures to defend the security of continental territory, internal waterbodies, territorial waters, and airspace, and to maintain national territorial sovereignty and maritime rights and interests.[12]

It is clear that the Chinese leadership sees maritime affairs as becoming a central part of the national interest. In order to secure those interests, Beijing is intent upon extending the reach of Chinese sovereignty, and to brook no opposition or challenge to that sovereignty. In this regard, Chinese behavior at sea parallels their efforts in other international common spaces. China is striving to compel others to accept its version of rules and behavior in what it calls "adjacent waters," much as it is intent upon getting others to accept its rules and behavior in cyberspace.

Chinese Political Warfare and the Maritime Domain

These efforts include the employment of political warfare. According to the People's Liberation Army (PLA), political warfare (*zhengzhi zuozhan*; 政治作战) is a form of combat (*douzheng fangshi*; 斗争方式) that encompasses all methods of non-military strikes. It is a type of political attack, which emphasizes political, theoretical, morale, and psychological means of conflict. It is a type of warfare that complements armed or kinetic combat, in that it seeks to achieve the same overall national strategic objectives, and is the responsibility of the armed forces. Thus, political warfare is not the same as robust diplomacy or economic pressure, although those measures may be applied as well. Instead, it might be best to characterize the Chinese view of political warfare as *the hardest form of soft power*.

In this context, the advent of the Information Age has allowed for the modernization, and especially the informationization, of political warfare. Information technology has created political combat styles under informationized conditions (*xinxi tiaojian xia de zhengzhi xing zuozhan yangshi*; 信息条件西

8. Hillary Clinton, Timothy Geitner, Dai Bingguo, and Wang Qishan, "Closing Remarks for US-China Strategic and Economic Dialogue," July 28, 2009, http://www.state.gov/secretary/20092013clinton/rm/2009a/july/126599.htm (accessed September 19, 2016).

9. State Oceanic Administration, Ocean Development Strategy Research Study Group, *China's Ocean Development Report, 2010* (Beijing, PRC: Maritime Publishing House, 2010), p. 469.

10. Charlie Zhu, "China Tests Troubled Waters with $1 Billion Rig for South China Sea," Reuters, June 21, 2012, http://www.reuters.com/article/us-china-southchinasea-idUSBRE85K03Y20120621 (accessed September 19, 2016).

11. "Xi Jinping at 8th CCP Politburo Study Session Emphasizes Attention to Maritime Affairs, Advancing Maritime Knowledge, Economic and Strategic Importance of the Maritime Domain, and Constantly Pushing Construction of a Strong Maritime Nation," *People's Daily*, August 1, 2013, http://paper.people.com.cn/rmrb/html/2013-08/01/nw.D110000renmrb_20130801_2-01.htm (accessed September 19, 2016).

12. National Security Law of the People's Republic of China, July 1, 2015, http://chinalawtranslate.com/2015nsl/?lang=en (accessed September 19, 2016).

的政治性作战样式). These entail the use of national and military resources, through the application of information technology, consistent with military strategic guidance, to secure the political initiative and psychological advantage over an opponent, in order to strengthen one's own will, gain allies, and debilitate an opponent.[13]

To accommodate the changes brought about by the proliferation of information technology, in 2003 the PLA issued the "Chinese People's Liberation Army Political Work Regulations (*zhongguo renmin jiefangjun zhengzhi gongzuo tiaoli;* 中国人民解放军政治工作条例)." Under these regulations, which were further updated in 2010, the PLA is tasked with the conduct of the "three warfares" of public opinion warfare, psychological warfare, and legal warfare. As PLA analyses note, the "three warfares" are a statement of the "operational function of political work (*zhengzhi gongzuo zuozhan gongneng;* 政治工作作战功能)." In effect, the "three warfares" constitute *the operationalization of political warfare.*

Within this context, the three warfares are intended to shape and mold the perceptions of three main audiences:

1. **The adversary's military and population.** This is a fundamental target for Chinese political warfare, with the aim of eroding both popular support and military morale. The Chinese not only draw upon their experiences with political warfare against the Nationalists in the Chinese Civil War, but also political warfare efforts in Vietnam and elsewhere. Chinese analysts have studied and discussed the impact of political warfare in the Iraq War and the Balkan conflicts.

2. **The domestic audience.** This includes the military and also the broader general population. PRC assessments of recent conflicts, including the Balkan wars of the 1990s and the 2003 Iraq War, concluded that an adversary may be able to achieve victory by undermining popular support or eroding military morale. Therefore, it is essential to build and sustain public support for a conflict.

3. **Third parties.** In today's interconnected world, the Chinese believe it is also essential to influence third-party political and military leaders, and the broader population. Garnering the sympathy and support of third parties is essential, both in strengthening one's own morale as well as undermining the adversary's. As important, it can lead to more substantive support, such as efforts to break sanctions or access to third-party assets.

Political warfare is the purview of the Political Work Department (PWD), one of the general departments that oversees the Chinese military. This organizational structure is important, because it is essential to recognize that the PWD is a key bureaucratic element of the PLA. Thus, political warfare will have a strong advocate for its implementation from a bureaucratic perspective. Given the emphasis upon engaging in political warfare as one would any other military campaign (i.e., with unity of command, clarity of objectives, concentration of resources, and coordination of activities), assigning one of the central bureaucracies of the PLA to manage such activities ensures that it is accorded as much importance and priority as more kinetic military activities.

Similarly, it is also vital to keep in mind that all aspects of political warfare, including the "three warfares," are ongoing in peacetime. One cannot successfully shape an adversary or third-party views, or credibly defend one's own populace, if one waits until the commencement of hostilities to undertake psychological, public opinion, or even legal warfare efforts. There must be preparation of the political battlefield, comparable to physical or intelligence preparation. Indeed, political warfare efforts are ongoing even in the absence of armed conflict.

An essential part of political warfare is legal warfare. From the Chinese perspective, legal warfare is not the "misuse" of the law, but rather, the exploitation of the law in support of broader political ends. As one Chinese volume notes:

> Regarding legal warfare, *it is necessary to abandon the perspectives of "real use of law" or "legal tools."* One must approach the issue from a "talking politics" perspective to understand the application of the legal weapon. One must start from national perspectives, people's highest will and basic interests, and under the guidance of the Party and the national guidelines of policy, use legal combat to achieve the political initiative [in war].[14]

---

13. Academy of Military Sciences Operations Theory and Regulations Research Department and Informationalized Operations Theory Research Office, *Informationalized Operations Theory Study Guide* (Beijing, PRC: AMS Press, November, 2005), p. 403.

14. Song Yunxia, *Legal Warfare Under Informationalized Conditions* (Beijing, PRC: AMS Publishing, 2007) (emphasis added).

The view that legal warfare supports broader military operations in attaining key national goals reinforces the importance of conducting legal warfare activities prior to the onset of hostilities and continuing afterwards. This pre-war "preparation of the battlefield" and post-conflict legal maneuverings, like wartime legal warfare activities, are aimed at fulfilling larger strategic goals.

In this regard, Chinese writers discuss the importance of preparing the legal battlefield, much as it is essential to undertake preparations of the physical battlefield. Such preparations include the creation of legal experts, which encompasses not only military lawyers, but as important, establishing a cadre of internationally recognized legal scholars, whose opinions will have weight abroad as well as at home.[15]

Such efforts also exploit not only the law, but also law enforcement agencies. For example, the use of the China Coast Guard (CCG) to enforce Chinese claims over the Senkakus, the Spratlys, and Scarborough Shoal not only serves to limit the potential for escalation, but also is a political statement. China is using law enforcement vessels to enforce *its* laws over *its* territories, reinforcing its claim to these various features.

Chinese Hard Power and the Maritime Domain

China is not solely relying upon political warfare methods to safeguard its interests in the maritime domain, however. The People's Liberation Army (PLA) has also been charged with the task. Since political warfare is seen as a form of warfare, and much of it is conducted in coordination with the military, this should be seen as a spectrum of effort, spanning less violent means (political warfare) to potentially more violent ones (kinetic operations). What is central is that all such measures are undertaken in support of a given set of strategic goals, and are coordinated with each other.

In this regard, the top Chinese leadership reiterated the need for the PLA to uphold Chinese interests in the maritime domain in 2004. At that time, then–General Secretary and Central Military Commission (CMC) chairman Hu Jintao charged the PLA with its "missions for the new stage of the new century," also referred to as its "new historic missions." Hu made clear that, in the more globalized world of the 21st century, Chinese interests could no longer be confined to homeland defense. Instead, because of

China's links to the rest of the world, it now had interest in the maritime, outer space, and electromagnetic domains. It would be the responsibility of the PLA to ensure that those interests were not molested.

To this end, the Chinese leadership has devoted substantial resources to modernizing and improving the PLA Navy (PLAN). China has long had the largest navy (in terms of number of hulls), but for several decades they were largely obsolete and of very limited range. This has been changing since the 1990s, however. From a largely coastal defense force, the PLA has been transformed. Today's PLAN fields a growing fleet of surface combatants capable of sustained operations away from its shores, and now includes an aircraft carrier, with at least one and perhaps three more apparently under construction. Its submarine arm has replaced many of its older, noisier platforms with quieter boats, some employing air-independent propulsion. China's navy spends more time at sea, with many of its surface combatant commanders now having served at least one mission in the Gulf of Aden. There is an indispensable annual U.S. Department of Defense report to Congress on Chinese military capability that provides extensive information on the specific Chinese platforms and capabilities now available to PLA planners.

As important, China's conception of naval operations has steadily expanded. From "near-shore operations," which roughly equate with coastal and brown-water duties, it has shifted emphasis to "near-sea" and now "far-sea" operations, roughly comparable to green water and blue water activities, respectively. These operations are not necessarily power projection–oriented, however.

The shift of China's economic center of gravity to its coast, as noted earlier, means that Beijing is at least as interested in keeping foreign air and naval forces away from China's shores. Indeed, Chinese anti-access/area denial (A2/AD) activities should be seen at least partly in this light. Given the range of modern precision-guided munition weapons, however, keeping an adversary away from China's shores means being able to undertake A2/AD activities at ranges of a thousand miles or more.

To this end, China is likely to employ not only traditional naval forces, but civilian and commercial assets, in unorthodox ways that embody "hybrid" approaches to warfare. China's fishing fleets, for example, include a substantial number of naval militia assets, essentially civilian vessels that respond

---

15. Yang Chunchang and Shen Hetai, Chief Editors, *Political Operations Under Informationalized Conditions* (Beijing, PRC: Long March Press, 2005).

to government (including military) assignments as necessary. Such forces could be exploited to provide everything from intelligence gathering to early warning for China's navy.[16] CCG vessels, some of which were cascaded from the PLAN, can do the same. More disturbingly, China has reportedly installed radars typically found on patrol vessels on some of the oil rigs in the East China Sea.[17] This further blurs the line between military and civilian assets, and suggests a new means by which oil rigs can serve as "mobile national territory," while further expanding China's maritime situational awareness envelope.

The South China Sea

The South China Sea is emblematic of these various Chinese concerns and responses. The waters bounded by China, Vietnam, Malaysia and Indonesia, and the Philippines and Taiwan have become a clear area of contention. For Beijing, a range of interests are at stake.

In the first place, there are significant natural resources within this area. The most important is *fish*. The fishing grounds of the South China Sea are some of the richest in the world, accounting for 12 percent of the global catch.[18] The Chinese ability to retain control over these waters and their bounty is part of the broader "food security" issue, which has long been a concern for Chinese leaders, and is exacerbated by China's growing dependence on imported food to meet the demands of its increasingly affluent population.

Another valuable resource is *hydrocarbons*. It has long been postulated that there are significant oil and gas deposits under the South China Sea. Given growing Chinese dependence on imported energy, the ability to access oil and natural gas immediately

offshore would be very appealing to Beijing. How much oil and gas may be under the surface is unclear. A 2010 U.S. Geological Survey fact sheet suggests that there are almost certainly at least reserves of 750 million barrels, and a median chance of 2 billion barrels in the South China Sea Platform area alone.[19]

The *physical space* of the South China Sea region itself is an invaluable resource, as it provides a strategic buffer. This is especially important as the PRC has built up the island of Hainan in the northwest corner of the South China Sea. Chinese military engineers have constructed a dock to handle its aircraft carriers, dedicated port facilities, including tunnels, for submarines, and a number of military airfields.[20] (The American EP-3 that collided with a Chinese fighter in 2001 crash-landed at one of these airfields.) In addition, China's newest spaceport is located on Hainan Island, where it will be lofting future manned Chinese space missions. It is clearly not in the Chinese interest to allow foreign, and especially American, naval capability to make close approaches to Hainan.

Instead, it is in China's interest to make the South China Sea as forbidding as possible, especially for American submarines, which remain qualitatively superior to their Chinese counterparts. It is therefore not surprising that there appears to be an effort to create a massive sonar surveillance network that would cover the region.[21] Indeed, military bases on the artificial islands China has built in the Spratlys, as well as in the Paracels and perhaps at Scarborough Shoal and Macclesfield Bank in the future, could provide convenient sites for processing data, and also for basing anti-submarine warfare aircraft and helicopters. Such deployments would make the deployment of American submarines into those waters far riskier.

16. Andrew Erickson and Conor M. Kennedy, "China's Maritime Militia: What It Is and How to Deal With It," *Foreign Affairs* (June 23, 2016), https://www.foreignaffairs.com/articles/china/2016-06-23/chinas-maritime-militia (accessed September 19, 2016)

17. "Japan Protests Over Chinese Radar in Disputed East China Sea Drilling Rig," *The Guardian* (U.K.), August 7, 2016, https://www.theguardian.com/world/2016/aug/07/japan-protests-over-chinese-radar-in-disputed-east-china-sea-drilling-rig (accessed September 19, 2016).

18. Trefor Moss, "Five Things About Fishing in the South China Sea," *Wall Street Journal Blog*, July 19, 2016, http://blogs.wsj.com/briefly/2016/07/19/5-things-about-fishing-in-the-south-china-sea/ (accessed September 19, 2016).

19. Christopher Schenk et. al., "Assessment of Undiscovered Oil and Gas Resources of Southeast Asia, 2010," U.S. Geological Survey, http://pubs.usgs.gov/fs/2010/3015/pdf/FS10-3015.pdf (accessed September 19, 2016).

20. David S. McDonough, "Unveiled: China's New Naval Base in the South China Sea," *The National Interest*, March 20, 2015, http://nationalinterest.org/blog/the-buzz/unveiled-chinas-new-naval-base-the-south-china-sea-12452 (accessed September 19, 2016), and Zachary Keck, "China Builds World's Largest Carrier Dock in South China Sea," *The National Interest*, July 31, 2015, http://nationalinterest.org/blog/the-buzz/china-builds-worlds-largest-aircraft-carrier-dock-south-13466 (accessed September 19, 2016).

21. Richard D. Fisher Jr., "China Proposes 'Underwater Great Wall' That Could Erode US, Russian Submarine Advantages," *Jane's Defence Weekly*, May 17, 2016, http://www.janes.com/article/60388/china-proposes-underwater-great-wall-that-could-erode-us-russian-submarine-advantages (accessed September 19, 2016).

Within this context, the findings of the Permanent Court of Arbitration (PCA) at the Hague regarding Chinese behavior in the South China Sea present the PRC with a problem. The PCA's willingness to hear the case, brought by the Republic of the Philippines in 2012, was itself a loss for China. Beijing has insisted that the PCA had no grounds for even taking the case, although both the Philippines and the PRC are signatories to the U.N. Convention on the Law of the Sea (UNCLOS), which calls for arbitration by the PCA in disputes, such as that brought by the Philippines.

The PCA's conclusions further damaged Chinese legal warfare and public opinion warfare efforts. Perhaps most centrally, the Court concluded that China's "9-dash line," which Beijing regularly references with regard to its claims in the South China Sea, does not grant the PRC any special rights in those waters. The Court also ruled on the legal status of each of the terrain features in the Spratly Islands area that the Philippines had incorporated in its case. In doing so, it concluded that none of them is, in fact, an "island" in the legal sense, and therefore none are entitled to a 200-nautical-mile exclusive economic zone (EEZ). At most, the Court said, some merit a 12-nautical-mile territorial sea zone.

The Court went on to determine that, as some areas of the South China Sea are within the Philippines EEZ (measured from the main Philippine archipelago), Chinese activities had violated Philippine sovereign rights. This included the construction of artificial islands (a major source of concern). In short, China's legal standing for its actions in the South China Sea, within the context of the UNCLOS, were minimal.

The Chinese reaction to these findings was remarkably intemperate. Chinese Foreign Minister Wang Yi described it as "political farce."[22] China's ambassador to the United States, Cui Tiankai, declared that the tribunal's failure to recognize its lack of jurisdiction was "a matter of professional incompetence," and raised questions of the court's integrity.[23] It is clear that Beijing has no intention of abiding by the PCA's rulings.

This rejection was underscored in the course of the recent G-20 summit, held in Hangzhou, China. Even before the summit was concluded, Filipino officials claimed that China was sending barges and other vessels to the disputed Scarborough Shoal.[24] The PCA had noted that the Chinese were violating Philippine rights when they interfere with Filipino fishermen around Scarborough Shoal.[25] That China would deliberately undertake activities in the midst of the G-20 summit suggests an effort to not only make clear Beijing's refusal to accept the PCA's findings, but to do so in front of a global audience.

Prospects for the Future

For the foreseeable future, tension in the Asian maritime environment is likely to rise. There is little reason to think that the PRC will become less dependent upon the seas, even if its economic activity should slow down. China is likely to remain dependent upon imports of raw materials and energy, and will continue to emphasize exports as a means of maintaining economic growth. As important, it is likely to continue to rely upon the sea for key foodstuffs, whether it is imports of agricultural products or fishing.

At the same time, the overhaul of the PLA, including the introduction of new services and the reorganization of the seven military regions into five war zones, is intended to make the PLA more capable of conducting "informationized local wars." As important, the PLA remains responsible for fulfilling the "new historic missions," including the defense of Chinese maritime interests.

China's ongoing activities in the South China Sea also indicate that there is little prospect of a reprieve in the area. Indeed, Chinese actions, including the construction of hardened aircraft shelters on the artificial islands in the Spratlys, make clear that it is paving the way for additional military options, if

22. "Chinese Foreign Minister Says South Sea Arbitration a Political Farce," Xinhua, July 13, 2016, http://news.xinhuanet.com/english/2016-07/13/c_135508275.htm (accessed September 19, 2016).

23. Chen Weihua, "China Envoy Blasts Hague Ruling," China Daily, July 13, 2016, http://usa.chinadaily.com.cn/epaper/2016-07/13/content_26071163.htm (accessed September 19, 2016).

24. Emily Rauhala, "During G-20, Philippines Spots More Chinese Ships Near Disputed Shoal," The Washington Post, September 5, 2016, https://www.washingtonpost.com/world/during-g20-philippines-spots-more-chinese-ships-near-disputed-shoal/2016/09/05/4970d7da-733d-11e6-a914-5d61c1ac8237_story.html (accessed September 19, 2016).

25. Robert D. Williams, "Tribunal Issues Landmark Ruling in South China Sea Arbitration," Lawfare (blog), July 12, 2016, https://www.lawfareblog.com/tribunal-issues-landmark-ruling-south-china-sea-arbitration (accessed September 19, 2016).

necessary. This will mark a substantial escalation, as Chinese activities have generally been presented as civilian, rather than military. It also belies President Xi Jinping's statement to President Obama that "relevant construction activity that China is undertaking in the Nansha [Spratly] Islands does not target or impact any country and there is no intention to militarize."[26]

In the coming months, it is therefore possible, even probable, that the PRC will undertake various measures to underscore its continued commitment to uphold and enforce its claims in the East and South China Seas. One action would be to begin undertaking reclamation efforts at Scarborough Shoal and the Macclesfield Bank area. In combination with the Spratlys and Paracels, this would allow the Chinese to encompass the entire "9-dash line" portion of the South China Sea within a dense sensor coverage umbrella. American and other nations attempting to operate air and naval forces in the international waters there would be under constant surveillance, and could be subjected to a variety of regular harassment.

Reclamation at Scarborough Shoal and Macclesfield Bank could therefore set the stage for the creation of a South China Sea air defense identification zone (ADIZ), similar to the East China Sea ADIZ that Beijing established in 2013. While the declaration of ADIZs, in and of themselves, are part of international behavior, China clearly views ADIZs much as it views maritime exclusive economic zones, i.e., as an extension of territorial airspace, rather than slight limitations on international airspace. Thus, China demands that aircraft flying through the East China Sea ADIZ conform to Chinese reporting requirements even if they are not entering Chinese airspace, or headed in that direction (e.g., surveillance and reconnaissance flights that are paralleling Chinese shores).[27] The creation of multiple military air bases, surface-to-air missile sites, and radar stations in the South China Sea would allow China to enforce a de facto South China Sea ADIZ, whether it formally declared one or not.

Similarly, as China's naval and air capabilities modernize, it is likely that there will also be more potential for encounters in the East China Sea. In the past month, China has dispatched several hundred fishing boats into the waters around the disputed Senkaku Islands. As important, CCG vessels were identified in the midst of these fishing boat flotillas, reflecting government support for these actions. Coupled with the apparent installation of patrol boat radars on oil rigs, this represents a steady escalation of capabilities—and potential for miscalculation.

The overall Chinese effort appears to be consistent with a desire to dominate the East Asian littoral within the first island chain (which stretches from the Japanese Home Islands through the Senkakus and Taiwan, the Philippines, Malaysia, and Indonesia). Within the area bounded by that chain, the Chinese are attempting to create a correlation of forces that would be in their favor. This includes establishing thorough, constant situational awareness through overlapping sensors, as well as the ability to bring a variety of weapons, from anti-ship ballistic missiles to cruise missiles to strike aircraft, anti-submarine warfare platforms, and air, surface, and subsurface combatants to bear.

****

26. David Brunnstrom and Michael Martina, "Xi Denies China Turning Artificial Islands into Military Bases," Reuters, September 25, 2015, http://www.reuters.com/article/us-usa-china-pacific-idUSKCN0RP1ZH20150925 (accessed September 19, 2016).

27. Matthew Waxman, "China's ADIZ at One Year: International Legal Issues," CSIS Asia Maritime Transparency Initiative, November 25, 2014, https://amti.csis.org/chinas-adiz-at-one-year-international-legal-issues/ (accessed September 19, 2016).

CONGRESSIONAL TESTIMONY

Members of The Heritage Foundation staff testify as individuals discussing their own independent research. The views expressed are their own and do not reflect an institutional position for The Heritage Foundation or its board of trustees.

———————

Mr. SALMON. Thank you.

Dr. Searight.

STATEMENT OF AMY SEARIGHT, PH.D., SENIOR ADVISER AND DIRECTOR, SOUTHEAST ASIA PROGRAM, CENTER FOR STRATEGIC AND INTERNATIONAL STUDIES

Ms. SEARIGHT. Thank you so much for this opportunity to talk about regional reactions to the Arbital Tribunal ruling.

Just a little bit over 2 months ago on July 12th, the Arbital Tribunal, under the United Nations Convention on the Law of the Sea, or UNCLOS, issued its landmark ruling in the case brought by the Philippines against China involving maritime rights and entitlements in the South China Sea.

In the weeks and months that have followed, the reaction to the ruling by the parties involved and others have played out more or less as expected.

But what was very unexpected was the breadth and the decisiveness of the ruling itself, which delivered an overwhelming legal victory to the Philippines and, by logical extension, to other claimants in the South China Sea in a decisive legal defeat to China.

In essence, the ruling does four things. First, it ruled that China's nine-dash line is not consistent with the Law of the Sea and invalidated Beijing's claims to historic rights throughout the nine-dash line.

Second, features in the South China Sea are, at most, entitled to only 12 nautical mile territorial zones and do not generate 200-mile exclusive economic zones or continental shelves.

Third, the panel found that China infringed on the traditional fishing rights of Filipinos by not allowing them to fish at Scarborough Shoal.

And fourth, the tribunal held that China's in violation of its obligations under UNCLOS to preserve and protect the marine environment, finding that it created massive environmental damage through its reclamation activities.

Now, the reactions to the ruling were very much predictable and predicated in most ways. China reacted swiftly and predictably, denouncing the tribunal as unjust and unlawful, declaring the award as null and void and has no binding force.

And Former State Counselor Dai Bingguo, in a visit to DC just before the ruling, said that the ruling would be treated as just a piece of trash paper.

The international community, led by the United States, including Japan, Australia, New Zealand and Canada, all put out very strong statements underscoring that the ruling was final and legally binding on both parties.

And, also of note, India put out a relatively strong statement as well. The ASEAN reactions to the ruling were also rather predictable, with Vietnam, Singapore, Malaysia and, somewhat surprisingly, Myanmar, using language that originated in the Sunnylands declaration in support for resolving disputes peacefully through "diplomatic and legal processes" in accordance with international law and UNCLOS.

Indonesia and Thailand also put out statements that were somewhat less robust, and the Philippines gave a very low-key response to its resounding legal victory. President Duterte had previously signaled that he wanted to move toward a soft landing with China.

So, Manila signaled its willingness to move forward to find a way forward toward talks to resolve the disputes and President Duterte dispatched Former President Fidel Ramos to Hong Kong to meet with Chinese officials.

These talks did not appear to yield any real progress, and there is still a major disagreement between the Philippines and China over whether the ruling should be the basis for any talks to resolve competing claims.

Duterte has also done a number of things, as Chairman Salmon elucidated. He has made clear that he wants the Philippines to have a more independent foreign policy. But what that precisely means I think is still being—still being played out.

The ASEAN reaction as a whole, as a grouping, ASEAN failed to project real unity in its response. It did not release a joint statement in the immediate aftermath.

It did have a joint communique that was issued 2 weeks later when the foreign ministers of ASEAN met in Vientiane, Laos, and this joint communique had a very long section on the South China Sea, which acknowledged concerns by some ministers on land reclamation and escalation of activities at sea which have eroded trust and confidence, increased tensions and may undermine peace, security and stability in the region.

So this was a way of providing an out to countries like Cambodia, which did not want to be on the record expressing concerns while giving voice to some of the concerns from Vietnam, the Philippines and others.

The communique also used the Sunnylands language of ''full respect for legal and diplomatic processes'' but, interestingly, it lifted this language out of the section on the South China Sea, and put it in the introductory section of the joint communique, reportedly at the request of Cambodia.

So as—you know, once again, this kind of revealed that ASEAN is a glass half empty and a glass half full in terms of its ability to deal with this issue and stand as a counterweight to China.

It is easy to be disappointed with the ASEAN, but I think it is very important to continue the engagement. We have seen repeatedly the positive effects that the President's engagement at Sunnylands has had on the grouping and their ability to signal some limited degree of unity and cohesion on this issue.

Secretary Carter is hosting the 10 ASEAN defense ministers in Hawaii next week, and it'll be very interesting to see what comes out of that.

Obviously, the most important factor in terms of how the impact of the ruling will have will be very much about how China will respond.

But let me just say three quick words about what role the United States can play.

First, the United States should continue to visibly demonstrate that it will continue to fly, sail and operate wherever international law allows by conducting regular freedom of navigation operations and other presence operations in the South China Sea.

Second, the United States should continue and accelerate capacity-building and training under the Maritime Security Initiative, foreign military financing and IMET. This is critical for enhancing capabilities of our key partners such as the Philippines, Vietnam, Indonesia and Malaysia and increasing interoperability with U.S. forces.

And, finally ratifying UNCLOS would be a very positive step to take as well. The ruling of the Arbital Tribunal panel and regional reactions to the ruling cast a glaring light on the mismatch between U.S. rhetoric, on the importance of upholding international law and the need for all countries to be bound by rules and norms and the fact that the United States has not yet ratified the treaty.

Simply put, our failure to ratify the treaty undermines our ability to fully work with our allies and partners in the South China Sea and insist that UNCLOS be used as a basis for resolving claims and arbitrating disputes.

China says this quite loudly in the region. But I would note that other countries say this more quietly as well.

[The prepared statement of Ms. Searight follows:]

CSIS | CENTER FOR STRATEGIC & INTERNATIONAL STUDIES

Statement before the

House Foreign Affairs

Subcommittee on Asia and the Pacific

"Diplomacy and Security in the South China Sea: After the Tribunal"

A Testimony by:

Dr. Amy Searight

Senior Adviser and Director, Southeast Asia Program
Center for Strategic and International Studies (CSIS)

September 22, 2016

2255 Rayburn House Office Building

Two months ago, on 12 July 2016, the Arbitral Tribunal under the United Nations Convention on the Law of the Sea (UNCLOS) issued its landmark ruling in the case brought by the Philippines against China involving maritime rights and entitlements in the South China Sea. In the weeks that followed reactions to the ruling by the parties and others have played out more or less as anticipated. What was very unexpected however was the breadth and decisiveness of the ruling itself, which delivered an overwhelming legal victory to the Philippines—and by logical extension to other claimants in the South China Sea—and a decisive legal defeat to China.

The five judges on the tribunal panel ruled unanimously in favor of the Philippines on 14 of the 15 claims it had brought against China. In essence the ruling did four things. First, the judges ruled that China's nine-dash line was not consistent with the Law of the Sea, and found that any claim China makes in the South China Sea must be made based on maritime entitlements from land features. The ruling invalidated Beijing's claims to historic rights throughout the nine-dash line, saying that any historic rights China might once have claimed in what are now the exclusive economic zones (EEZs) or continental shelves of other countries were invalidated by UNCLOS.

Second, the tribunal found that features in South China Sea claimed by both China and the Philippines generate at most only 12 nautical mile (nm) territorial zones, and do not generate 200 mile exclusive economic zones (EEZs) or continental shelves. This means that China has no EEZ overlap with the Philippines, nor does it have a legal basis for claiming EEZ overlaps with Malaysia, Indonesia, or Brunei. This dramatically minimizes the scope of legally valid disputes.

Third, the tribunal ruled that China infringed on the traditional fishing rights of Filipinos by not allowing them to fish at Scarborough Shoal. Interestingly, the judges also noted that had the situation been reversed and the Philippines had prevented Chinese fisherman access to Scarborough Shoal, that also would be a violation by the Philippines. By logical extension, all countries that have historically fished in the area, which includes Taiwanese and Vietnamese fisherman, also have legally valid claims to maintain access to lawful fishing activities at the shoal, and the Philippines made the point during their legal arguments that those traditional rights were respected by the Philippines when it controlled and administered Scarborough Shoal until April 2012.[i]

Fourth, in one of the most legally significant parts of the ruling, the judges ruled that China in violation of its obligations under UNCLOS to preserve and protect the marine environment, finding that it created massive environmental damage through its reclamation activities on features in the South China Sea that destroyed pristine coral reefs, and that these large-scale reclamation and construction activities in addition to damaging Chinese fishing practices had decimated fragile marine ecosystems. According to legal scholars, these findings mark a significant step in the clarification of the environmental protection provisions of UNCLOS, and could boost efforts to apply these obligations more widely among states, in the South China Sea and beyond.[ii]

In sum, this was a deep and conclusive ruling that sweeps away a vast amount of ambiguity on questions surrounding the validity of China's maritime claims, the status of features under UNCLOS, and the strength of the environmental protections under UNCLOS.

Responses to the arbitral tribunal ruling

China reacted swiftly and predictably to the ruling, denouncing the tribunal as "unjust and unlawful" and declaring the award "is null and void and has no binding force." Just before the ruling during a visit to Washington, former Chinese state councilor Dai Bingguo said that the ruling would be "just a piece of trash paper." China also quickly announced some symbolic military maneuvers, including naval exercises off of Hainan and combat air patrols over the South China Sea, as well as landing of a civilian aircraft for the first time on Mischief Reef. Overall however China's actions to date have been somewhat restrained. Many observers had expected China to refrain from provocative actions until after it hosted the G-20 in Hangzhou in early September, but China appears to be continuing to exercise relative restraint, perhaps to avoid becoming a target of political debate in the run-up to the U.S. presidential election.

Reactions from the international community also played out more or less according to script. The United States, Japan, Australia and New Zealand issued strong statements underscoring that the ruling was final and legally binding on both parties. Of note, India also issued a relatively strong statement supporting the ruling and calling for UNCLOS to be respected, noting that India along with several ASEAN states have abided by rulings handed down by the International Tribunal in previous cases.[iii]

ASEAN and individual Southeast Asian countries
Most countries in Southeast Asia have responded rather cautiously to the ruling. In addition to the Philippines, Indonesia, Malaysia, Myanmar, Singapore, Thailand, and Vietnam have issued official statements on the ruling.

Malaysia, Singapore, Vietnam, and, surprisingly, Myanmar, have expressed their support for the resolution of disputes through peaceful means, including diplomatic and legal processes, and in accordance with international law and UNCLOS.[iv] Singapore and Vietnam indicated that they are studying the content of the ruling. Vietnam went a step further to reiterate that it "strongly supports" the "maintenance of [...] freedoms of navigation and over-flight" in the sea. Notably, Vietnam also reaffirmed its previous statements on the arbitration, including its submission to the tribunal which, among other things, recognized the judges' jurisdiction.

Indonesia called on all parties to resolve their disputes according to international law, including UNCLOS, but without any direct reference to the arbitration.[v] And Thailand issued a statement ahead of the ruling that urged for peace and stability in the South China Sea, and called on all parties to exercise self-restraint.[vi]

The Philippines had a notably low key response to its resounding legal victory, reflecting the new direction that newly inaugurated President Rodrigo Duterte had signaled he wanted to move toward a "soft landing" with China.[vii] Foreign Secretary Perfecto Yasay welcomed the ruling and called on all parties "to exercise restraint and sobriety," adding the following day that "we cannot gloat about our triumphs."[viii] Manila also signaled it would be willing to begin quiet talks with Beijing seeking a *modus vivendi* to manage disputes. However, when China sought to precondition talks on excluding any consideration of the legal ruling, Manila made clear that it would insist that talks must be based on the verdict.

In August, President Duterte dispatched a special envoy, former Philippine president Fidel Ramos, to Hong Kong to meet with current and former Chinese officials as an "ice breaker" to explore grounds for talks between the two sides. The visit did not appear to lead to any tangible results or a clear way forward. Chinese officials continue to reject any talks that are launched on the basis of the ruling, but they have invited Ramos to Beijing for further discussion.

ASEAN as a whole failed to project any unity over its response to the arbitral tribunal ruling. Two weeks after the ruling, ASEAN foreign ministers convened in Vientiane, Laos for the ASEAN Regional Forum meetings, and they discussed recent developments in the South China Sea. In the joint communiqué they issued at the meeting, the ASEAN ministers made no mention of the outcomes of the ruling, but they did devote significant attention to the issue by ASEAN standards. Of note, they acknowledged concerns expressed by "some ministers" on land reclamation and escalation of activities in the sea, which they said "have eroded trust and confidence, increased tensions and may undermine peace, security and stability in the region." The "some ministers" formulation was a way to give voice to ASEAN members that have increasingly strong concerns, such as Vietnam and the Philippines, while giving an out to members like Cambodia who do not want to express such concern about China. Also of note was the fact that the language included in the Sunnylands Declaration of "full respect for legal and diplomatic processes" was lifted out of the section on the South China Sea and put into the introductory section, reportedly at Cambodia's insistence. [ix] The section on the South China Sea in the July communiqué was the longest ever devoted to the South China Sea issue in official ASEAN meetings, and yet by pulling punches it perfectly reflects the glass half-full, glass half-empty nature of ASEAN's ability to deal with this issue and stand as a counterweight to China. ASEAN is both essential for bringing moral pressure to bear on China, but also is, and probably always will be, a very imperfect vessel for expressing unity and cohesion on this issue.

ASEAN at a crossroads

The South China Sea continues to be a divisive issue within ASEAN. While it is not the single most important issue on the grouping's agenda, it is often the most difficult issue around which to forge consensus among all member states—the principle on which ASEAN operates. China has been able to use its economic patronage to peel away Cambodia and sometimes Laos from ASEAN consensus on the South China Sea at ASEAN meetings, making it difficult for ASEAN to forge an effective collective position on developments in the South China Sea.

The deadlock that ASEAN frequently encounters on the South China Sea issue has prompted a broader and more serious debate among its leaders about the "ASEAN Way," which favors consensus-building above all. ASEAN secretary-general Le Luong Minh announced earlier this month that he has received the mandate of all ASEAN foreign ministers to review and update the charter of ASEAN—which was adopted in 2007 and spells out the grouping's norms, rules, and values—in order to make it more efficient in the current environment. While the principle of consensus, which is enshrined in the charter, will not likely be modified since it helps ensure that no member state is marginalized on major decisions, he admitted that "very often it delays the very process of reaching that consensus."[x] Vietnamese president Tran Dai Quang recently suggested that "it is possible for countries of ASEAN to consider and supplement a number of other principles [...] to the principle of consensus in ASEAN" in order to address newly emerging issues—a clear reference to the South China Sea.[xi]

While there are structural forces that prevent ASEAN from speaking more cohesively on the South China Sea, the ruling offered the grouping an important equalizer in its engagement with China on the issue. China has said it neither accepts nor will abide by the ruling, yet its actions indicate that it at least recognizes that it needs to begin engaging ASEAN more substantively than in the past. After years of dragging its feet on talks for a binding Code of Conduct (COC) for parties in the South China Sea, China announced last month that it aims to conclude a framework for the COC with ASEAN in mid-2017. China and ASEAN also recently agreed to establish a hotline to manage maritime emergencies, and to employ the Code for Unplanned Encounters at Sea between their navies in the South China Sea—both initiatives had been put forward by ASEAN. While skeptics can rightly point to the extremely slow pace which China will likely continue to exhibit in implementing these initiatives, it is hard to imagine that China would have agreed to them without the pressure of the arbitral ruling.

The Philippines will chair ASEAN in 2017. To date, President Duterte's approach to the South China Sea has marked a stark shift from his predecessor. Under President Aquino the Philippines was a consistently strong voice in ASEAN meetings on South China Sea developments, but the current government has pulled back quite a bit from seeking ASEAN support on the issue. Other ASEAN members, in particular claimant states, recognize that this new dynamic could carry significant implications for their own interests and ASEAN's collective position, given the consensus principle that guides the grouping. Other states with claims or stakes in the South China Sea are not necessarily averse to Duterte's overtures to China in the aftermath of the ruling. However, they recognize that Manila's willingness to find common ground with China and be more confrontational with its ally, the United States, could in the process result in additional leverage for China and, in that event, force them to recalculate their own interests and approaches toward both Washington and Beijing.

The Impact of the Ruling

More than two months after the verdict was announced, government lawyers and diplomats across the region are still absorbing the 500-page ruling and its legal implications. Meanwhile strategists and legal scholars are debating its long-term impact. Will the dramatically altered legal landscape lead to significant behavioral changes among claimant states, and most importantly China? Or will China continue to flout the ruling, double-down on its defiant rejection, and seek to further change facts on the ground to support its maritime claims? Will the ruling be a game changer?[xii] Or a paper tiger?

In the proceedings at The Hague, then Philippine foreign secretary Alberto Del Rosario began his closing remarks by noting that "International law is the great equalizer among states. It allows small countries to stand on an equal footing with more powerful states. Those who think 'might makes right' have it backwards. It is exactly the opposite, in that right makes might." But as many observers and China itself were quick to point out, the tribunal does not have an army or police force to enforce its ruling. The ruling will only have an impact if the weight of world opinion, and the legitimacy of UNCLOS legal process, leads China eventually into grudging compliance. The Philippines' lead counsel for the case, Paul Reichler, predicts that it will. He has argued in the wake of the decisive ruling that this will ultimately lead China to seek to settle its disputes with other claimants through negotiations.[xiii] He points to the "reputational damage …and the loss of prestige and loss of influence with other states when you declare yourself an international outlaw, a state that doesn't care for or respect international law."[xiv] Reichler, who also served on the Nicaragua legal team in its 1980s dispute with the United States, notes that even in that case, although the United States defied the ICJ judgement, it ended up coming into substantial compliance after the publicity of the case led the U.S. Congress to cut off funding for the Contra rebels in 1988 and the U.S. lifted the trade embargo in 1990.[xv]

Ultimately the impact of the ruling will depend on a several key developments. The first is the role of domestic public opinion in the claimant states. The verdict provides a clear-cut legal case against excessive Chinese maritime claims and actions that infringe on Philippines' rights, and by logical extension this provides legal ammunition for other claimant states—Vietnam, Malaysia, and Brunei—as well as Indonesia, which has challenged China's fishing practices within its EEZ near its Natuna Islands, to push back on China's excessive claims and pursuant actions. Will the domestic publics of these states absorb and embrace the legal ruling and demand that their governments stand up to China? We have already seen strong public opinion in the Philippines in favor of the ruling push the Duterte government to take a somewhat firmer line with Beijing than the cooperative approach initially favored by Duterte. Indonesia, one of the architects of the UNCLOS treaty, reacted to the ruling with a muted response, leading several dozen Indonesian scholars to sign a letter calling for a more vigorous embrace of the ruling. Will nationalist public sentiment push governments in Indonesia, Malaysia and other countries to be more firm in response to incursions in their EEZs, and to insist on Chinese compliance with the ruling?

Second, and relatedly, will domestic and international environmental advocates seize on the environmental aspects of the ruling to further publicize/highlight the catastrophic impact of China's reclamation and fishing activities on the fragile marine ecosystem? To date, environmental non-governmental organizations (NGOs) have been remarkably silent on China's environmental destruction, which the court, citing biologist Kent Carpenter, said "constitutes the most rapid nearly permanent loss of coral reef area" ever caused by human activity.[xvi] But the ruling may lead to more calls from international NGOs and domestic groups to insist that joint management of resources and monitoring and protection of the marine environment is essential to preserve the maritime environmental commons, and is a legal obligation of states under UNCLOS.

Third, will claimant governments be encouraged by the ruling to file their own cases against China at the Permanent Court of Arbitration? Vietnam and Indonesia have each previously indicated that they were considering their own legal action against China, and the strong precedent set by this case could encourage them further down this legal path. On the other hand, the leverage that comes with the "threat" of bringing a legal claim against China to arbitration may be more useful to coax China to the negotiating table, or at minimum induce better behavior from China, rather than actually filing a claim at The Hague.

Fourth, and obviously most significant, is how China chooses to respond in the coming months and years. Will Beijing double-down on its defiant non-compliance, and seek to further change facts on the ground to support its position? Many observers expected that China would take steps in this direction immediately after the ruling, such as declaring an Air Defense Identification Zone (ADIZ) in the South China Sea, or moving to begin reclamation on Scarborough Shoal. So far China has restrained from these kinds of provocative actions, but several windows are worth watching for potential Beijing actions—including the period after China hosts the G-20 in Hangzhou in early September through the U.S. election and transition period in November-January, and then again in the early months of a new U.S. administration. If China wanted to "test the waters" when the U.S. government is constrained or less fully focused, these timeframes might seem tempting.

In the most optimistic scenario, over time China will nudge its claims in the South China Sea towards compliance with UNCLOS. Some observers have already seen some signs that they believe point to Chinese movement in this direction. Andrew Chubb, for example, highlights the degree to which Chinese leadership is now focusing on Chinese sovereignty over the features, which was not actually challenged in the arbitral tribunal ruling. "Driving attention towards this tough-sounding stance on territorial sovereignty provides good political cover for the quiet clarification of China's maritime rights claims that may be underway" he writes.[xvii]

Yet not even the most optimistic observers can expect China to come into full compliance of the tribunal ruling. Full compliance by China would seem to be nearly impossible to achieve, given that it would require them to abandon their facilities on Mischief Reef, which the tribunal determined was a low-tide elevation not entitled to maritime claims, and situated squarely within the Philippines' EEZ. Short of full compliance, then, what would "substantial compliance" look like? What could the international community realistically expect China to do in order to demonstrate that it is not flouting international law? I would suggest that if China clarifies the nine-dash line in a manner consistent with UNCLOS; quietly refrains from interfering with resource exploitation by other claimants within their own EEZs, and refrains more broadly from interfering with traditional fishing activities; and limits maritime law enforcement activities to the territorial waters of SCS features it controls, would constitute a case of "substantial compliance" that would mark a huge victory for international law and the weight of world opinion.

Finally, what role will the United States play? So far, the United States has sought to rally a strong diplomatic message to convey that world opinion is decidedly on the side of the legally binding nature of the UNCLOS-mandated tribunal ruling while providing some space for the Philippines to approach China for consultations towards a peaceful resolution of their dispute. Let me end with two recommendations for U.S. policy going forward. First, the United States needs to visibly demonstrate that it will continue to "fly, sail and operate wherever international law allows." This means continuing to conduct regular Freedom of Navigation Operations (FONOPs), and other presence operations, in the vicinity of these disputed features on a regular basis. FONOPs, which are a global program designed to challenge excessive maritime claims, and other presence activities should be a regular occurrence, and not something that is ratcheted up and then down in response to legal developments or short-term behavioral changes. They should not be seen as provocations, nor are they bargaining chips.

Second, the United States should continue its efforts to build capacity of key partners and allies, in particular the Philippines but also Vietnam, Indonesia, Malaysia, and Thailand. Stepping up efforts to accelerate capacity building through the Maritime Security Initiative (MSI) and Foreign Military Financing (FMF) and International Military Education and Training (IMET) will be critical to shape the regional environment in our favor.

And finally, perhaps the ruling will at long last lead the U.S. Senate to ratify UNCLOS. Although it has never ratified UNCLOS, the United States accepts the UN convention as customary international law. And yet the ruling of the arbitral tribunal panel, and regional reactions to the ruling, have cast a glaring light once again on the mismatch between what U.S. rhetoric on upholding international law and the need for all countries to be bound by rules and norms, and the fact that it has not ratified UNCLOS. For the weight of world opinion to have any chance of shaping China's behavior, ratifying UNCLOS is an important first step.

---

[i] Asia Maritime Transparency Initiative (AMTI), Podcast: Arbitration Outcomes with Paul Reichler, Philippines' Lead Counsel, Part 2, https://amti.csis.org/podcast-arbitration-outcomes-paul-reichler-philippines-lead-counsel/.

[ii] Julie Makinen, "China's Claims in South China Sea Are Invalid, Tribunal Rules, In Victory for the Philippines," *Los Angeles Times*, July 12, 2016, http://www.latimes.com/world/asia/la-fg-south-china-sea-ruling-20160712-snap-story.html; HerbertSmithFreehills Dispute Resolution, "Final Award Published in the South China Sea Arbitration," July 20, 2016, http://hsfnotes.com/publicinternationallaw/2016/07/20/final-award-published-in-the-south-china-sea-arbitration/; AMTI, Podcast, Arbitration Outcomes with Paul Reichler, Philippines' Lead Counsel, Part 2.

[iii] See http://mea.gov.in/Speeches-Statements.htm?dtl/27140. "In the context of the Award of the Arbitral Tribunal constituted under Annex VII of the 1982 UNCLOS in the matter concerning the Philippines and China, India, as a State Party to the UNCLOS, urges all parties to show utmost respect for the UNCLOS, which is the foundation of the international legal order of the seas and oceans. Like several ASEAN countries, India too has respected the decision of the International Tribunal to resolve maritime disputes with its neighbors peacefully. India believes that States should resolve disputes through peaceful means, without threat or use of force, and exercise self-restraint in the conduct of activities that could complicate or escalate disputes affecting peace and stability."

[iv] Ministry of Foreign Affairs of Malaysia, Statement by Malaysia Following the Decision on the Arbitral Tribunal on the South China Sea Issue (press release), http://www.kln.gov.my/web/ukr_kiev/home/-/asset_publisher/8pPT/blog/statement-by-malaysia-following-the-decision-of-the-arbitral-tribunal-on-the-south-china-sea-issue?redirect=%2Fweb%2Fukr_kiev%2Fhome; Ministry of Foreign Affairs of Singapore, MFA Spokesman's Comments on the Ruling of the Arbitral Tribunal in the Philippines v China Case Under Annex VII to the 1982 United Nations Convention on the Law of the Sea (press release), https://www.mfa.gov.sg/content/mfa/media_centre/press_room/pr/2016/201607/press_20160712_2.html; Ministry of Foreign Affairs of Vietnam, Remarks of the Spokesperson of the Ministry of Foreign Affairs of Viet Nam on Viet Nam's reaction to the issuance of the Award by the Tribunal constituted under Annex VII to the United Nations Convention on the Law of the Sea in the arbitration between the Philippines and China (press release), http://www.mofa.gov.vn/en/tt_baochi/pbnfn/ns160712211059/view; and Ministry of Foreign Affairs of Myanmar, Myanmar's Statement on the Award of the Arbitral Tribunal on the South China Sea under Annex VII of UNCLOS (press release), http://www.mofa.gov.mm/wp-content/uploads/2016/07/Press-Releases.pdf.

[v] Ministry of Foreign Affairs of Indonesia, Indonesia Calls on All Parties to Respect International Law Including UNCLOS 1982 (press release), http://www.kemlu.go.id/en/berita/Pages/Indonesia-Calls-On-All-Parties-To-Respect-International-Law-Including-UNCLOS-1982.aspx.

[vi] Ministry of Foreign Affairs of Thailand, Statement of Thailand on Peace, Stability and Sustainable Development in the South China Sea (press release), http://www.mfa.go.th/main/en/media-center/14/68341-Statement-of-Thailand-on-Peace,-Stability-and-Sust.html.

[vii] "Duterte to Seek 'Soft Landing' with China after Dispute Ruling," ABS-CBN News, June 30, 2016, http://news.abs-cbn.com/focus/06/30/16/duterte-to-seek-soft-landing-with-china-after-dispute-ruling.

[viii] Paterno Esmaquel, "PH-China Ruling: Why Yasay Wasn't Smiling," Rappler, July 13, 2016, http://www.rappler.com/newsbreak/inside-track/139620-yasay-somber-statement-philippines-china-ruling.

[ix] Prashanth Parameswaran, "Assessing ASEAN's South China Sea Position in its Post-Ruling Statement," The Diplomat, July 25, 2016, http://thediplomat.com/2016/07/assessing-aseans-south-china-sea-position-in-its-post-ruling-statement/.

[11] Tan Qiuyi, "ASEAN Charter under Review: ASEAN Secretary-General," Channel News Asia, September 7, 2016, http://www.channelnewsasia.com/news/asiapacific/asean-charter-under-review-asean-secretary-general/3108772.html.

[xi] "Asean Urged to Look beyond Consensus in Decision Making," *Bangkok Post*, August 30, 2016, http://www.bangkokpost.com/news/asean/1074425/asean-urged-to-look-beyond-consensus-in-decision-making.

[xii] Alexander L. Vuving, "Why the South China Sea Ruling Is a Game Changer," The Diplomat, July 27, 2016, http://thediplomat.com/2016/07/why-the-south-china-sea-ruling-is-a-game-changer/.

[xiii] Jane Perlez, "Defending David against the World's Goliaths in International Court," *New York Times*, July 15, 2016, http://www.nytimes.com/2016/07/16/world/asia/south-china-sea-philippines-hague.html.

[xiv] Asia Maritime Transparency Initiative, Podcast: Arbitration Outcomes with Paul Reichler, Philippines' Lead Counsel, Part 3, https://amti.csis.org/podcast-arbitration-outcomes-paul-reichler-philippines-lead-counsel/.

[xv] Lan Nguyen and Truong Minh Vu, "After the Arbitration: Does Non-Compliance Matter?," Asia Maritime Transparency Initiative, July 22, 2016, https://amti.csis.org/arbitration-non-compliance-matter/.

[xvi] Makinen, "China's Claims in South China Sea Are Invalid."

[xvii] Andrew Chubb, "Did China just clarify the nine-dash line?," East Asia Forum, July 14, 2016, http://www.eastasiaforum.org/2016/07/14/did-china-just-clarify-the-nine-dash-line/.

Mr. SALMON. Thank you.

Dr. Etzioni. Could you turn on your microphone? Thank you.

STATEMENT OF AMITAI ETZIONI, PH.D., PROFESSOR OF INTERNATIONAL AFFAIRS, DIRECTOR, INSTITUTE OF COMMUNITARIAN POLICY STUDIES, THE GEORGE WASH-INGTON UNIVERSITY

Mr. ETZIONI. Asking a professor to say anything in 5 minutes is absolute torture.

But thank you, Chairman Salmon, Ranking Member Sherman, distinguished members of the committee for tolerating a much less alarmed view of the situation and for the suggestion that we should see the questions of the contested islands in the context of the much larger question of the United States-China relationship.

If I had to say in one sentence what I'm trying to suggest is that the situation is particularly ripe for a grand bargain between the United States and China on all the outstanding issues.

The reason I argue that that on many, many issues, on most issues, is the United States and China have identical or complementary interests; therefore, the part which is left to be settled is relatively small.

These include the fact that both nations desperately need resources for very pressing domestic issues. I won't list them because they are terribly familiar.

But we tend to overlook that China also has enormously pressing domestic—hence, any additional deflection of resources needed for domestic rebuilding, to military, pressures both sides.

China, as the Paris Accord shows, is concerned about climate issues. Both nations are concerned about proliferation of nuclear weapons.

Both nations are concerned of jihadist terrorism. I cannot take more time. There is a long list of complementary and shared interests.

The remaining issues, in my judgment, should be approached in a very different manner, and this is not often discussed—I appreciate the opportunity to put it before you—and that is focusing on issues in which there is a high difference in saliency.

There are some issues which are very important to us and much less important to China and on those we should expect China to give way, and there are some issues that are very important to them and next to unimportant to us.

And a bargain arises here not by trading A for B's but by us giving in on things that don't matter to us in return for things very important to us. Let me give an example to make it much less abstract.

The number-one United States priority today is not who is going to fish where or who is going to build what on those rocks.

The number-one security challenge is, obviously, North Korea, which in a year or two could have long-range missiles equipped with nuclear weapons.

The only way short of an outright war, which would be extremely troubling, to get a handle on this is a collaboration with China.

That's something very important to us. China has no deep reason to avoid reining in Korea other than they face much higher costs than we if they do so.

So, if we are going to get China collaboration in reining in North Korea, we have to find out something which is important to them but not to us. And a great example is we don't need a missile shield in South Korea if the North Korea nuclear problem is defanged. China is very worried about it because it is not clear to them that the same shield will not stop their missiles.

So, here is a good example of giving up something we really basically don't need in return for something which worries them a great deal.

My second example would be the situation in Pakistan. Most security experts I know agree that the greatest threat as far as terrorism is concerned is if they get their hands on nuclear weapons in Pakistan, which are not under their control.

Some of them are on the front lines next to India under local control. There have been already six attempts by ISIS or al-Qaeda and other groups to get a hold of these nuclear weapons. I would like to add something here which is not often mentioned.

We control our airways, our interests in the United States and land quite well. Our seas are completely open. There are 2 million recreational vehicles that come and go at will. It would be extremely easy for a group of terrorists and a nuclear weapon to land at any one of our beaches.

So China has leverage with Pakistan, much more than we. We are arguing if you are going to give them $1 billion or not. China is pledging $25 billion. China has given them very large control of their armament and such.

So here is an example. We should be very interested in China joining us in reining in the nuclear programs of Pakistan. But, what in turn will speak to them, which is of very low cost to us, may involve reining in India.

I am running out of time here, but the basic principle is clear. You should see what's happening over the islands in the larger context, starting with most important to us, what is second most important to us, and see if there are not things which China can help us on these fronts, which they would be more than willing to do for giving them things which we are all too ready to get rid of.

Thank you very much.

[The prepared statement of Mr. Etzioni follows:]

Amitai Etzioni
Testimony before Asia and Pacific subcommittee
Diplomacy and Security in the South China Sea: After the Tribunal
September 22, 2016

Several American analysts point to the modernization of the Chinese military; its

development of anti-access, area denial capabilities; China's rapid economic growth; and its

expansionist conduct, especially the building up of some islands in the South China Sea—as

indications that sooner or later the US will go to war with China. They hence advocate increased

military budgets, placement of US troops and warships in the area, military alliances with nations

on the border of China, and drawing a redline when it comes to the contested islands.

As I see it, the Chinese military buildup is coming from a very low base, and is far from

approaching that of the US. The difference is highlighted by the fact that China now has one

aircraft carrier while the US has eleven. The anti-access, anti-ship missiles are mainly defensive

weapons, of concern for anybody who wants to attack China but otherwise do not threaten the

US or its allies. China's economic growth is slowing and its income per capita is and will be for

decades well below that of the US. It is close to that of El Salvador. The fate of the contested

islands should be settled as part of a much more all-encompassing bargain with China, rather

than turned into a major issue in its own right, a test of China's good character or of US

credibility and fortitude.

Above all, I note that the US and China have many shared and complementary interests

and very few real reasons for conflict. These shared interests include preventing the spread of

terrorism (obviously a major concern for the U.S. and its allies but also for China where Uighur

separatists have launched attacks against the government since the 1990s); non-proliferation of nuclear arms (China voted with the US in 2016 at the UN to board all ships on their way to or from North Korea to ensure that they do not carry nuclear materials); global financial stability; preventing the spread of pandemics; and environmental protection, in particular climate change. In addition, the US has a major interest in making major investments in nation building at home and not in continuing to increase military expenditures in preparing for a war with China.

The remaining issues can be settled best if both sides focus on the issues most important to them. The US' number one security risk in Asia is a North Korea armed with nuclear and chemical weapons, long range missiles, and an unpredictable dictator. If it attacks South Korea or Japan, the US will be dragged into a war, which it is sure to win but only after devastating costs to its allies and its status. China has the leverage to compel North Korea to change course, but it has to be incentivized to proceed because of the costs to itself of twisting North Korea's arms. This is the case because first, China fears that if the regime in Pyongyang collapses, many millions of North Koreans will flee into China, and it will have to accommodate them. Second, that following the unification of Korea, the US will move its troops to the border with China. It is hence not enough for the US to call on China or try to shame China into pressing North Korea to give up its nuclear arms buildup. First of all, it has to informally negotiate an agreement with China that the area that is now North Korea would not be occupied by either side and that the nuclear arms there now will be destroyed rather than added to China's arsenal. In return, the US has to commit itself to not placing a nuclear missile shield in South Korea. China has reasons to be concerned about such a shield because it could be used to undermine its nuclear deterrent. Other incentives may well be needed, for instance, stopping the near daily American intelligence flights up and down Chinese coastlines, which are of very limited use for the US and very antagonizing to China.

The second major US security interest in Asia is to ensure that terrorists are unable to get their hands on nuclear weapons in Pakistan (something they have already tried six times). Given that China is the primary source of arms and investments for Pakistan, this second US security objective may be achieved if, as part of the grand bargain, the US agrees to stop helping India develop its nuclear arsenal and stops pushing its military build-up to counter China.

Several additional examples follow. One may well dispute one or the other, but the main purpose is to illustrate elements of a grand bargain approach.

Clarifying Intentions Regarding Taiwan

Making explicit that which is viewed by many as an implicit understanding between China and the United States regarding the status of Taiwan would constitute a major step toward defusing tensions between the two powers. The governments of both the United States and China have already demonstrated considerable self-restraint in the matter of Taiwan. Beijing has not yielded to demands from those who call for employing force as a means of "reclaiming" Taiwan as part of the mainland; meanwhile, Washington has not yielded to Americans who urge the recognition of Taiwan as an independent country. These measures of self-restraint should be made more explicit by letting it be known that so long as China does not use force to coerce Taiwan to become part of China, the United States will continue to refrain from treating Taiwan as an independent state.

One may ask whether it is not best to let sleeping dogs lie. One reason to clarify both sides' policies is that hawks in both nations use the cause of Taiwan to justify building up the United States' and China's respective military forces in an era in which it is necessary for both nations to focus on economic, social, and environmental issues at home. A 2013 report to Congress from the Department of Defense concurs, stating, "Preparing for potential conflict in the Taiwan Strait appears to remain the principal focus and primary driver of China's military investment."[i] Moreover, China carried out a military exercise in which the PLA simulated "a Normandy-style invasion" of Taiwan.[ii] In the United States, a 2003 report from the Council on Foreign Relations examined China's growing military power and held that "minimizing the chances that a cross-strait crisis will occur means maintaining the clear ability and willingness to counter any application of military force against Taiwan."[iii]

Making an explicit commitment to maintain the status quo of Taiwan, unless the people of Taiwan freely and peacefully choose otherwise, would significantly reduce tensions between the United States and China.

Cyberspace

A grand bargain is particularly important for restraining the proliferation of weapons such as cyber arms that favor those who strike first. Such weapons are particularly destabilizing because they offer tangible incentives to strike before being struck, thereby increasing the probability that a country possessing them will escalate a situation. Cyber arms, roughly defined, are malicious computer programs designed to conduct espionage or to disable or destroy physical infrastructure. Because espionage has been a reality of international relations for as long as nations have existed and because "kinetic" cyber weapons remain rare, it seems likely that any new shared understandings of vetted self-restraint in the realm of information technology will center on those cyber tools capable of causing physical damage rather than those that collect intelligence.

A draft code that seeks to forestall conflicts involving cyber arms has already been proposed. In September 2011, four countries—China, Russia, Tajikistan, and Uzbekistan—submitted an "International Code of Conduct for Information Security" to UN Secretary-General

Ban Ki-moon. The draft calls for a "consensus on the international norms and rules standardizing the behavior of countries concerning information and cyberspace at an early date." The document further asks states to pledge "not to use [information and communication technologies] including networks to carry out hostile activities or acts of aggression and pose threats to international peace and security." [iv]

Critics have found fault in this draft, suggesting the draft may lead to increased state censorship and control of the Internet; however, these critics have failed to propose an alternate text. It seems more constructive to amend and modify the suggested text rather than to dismiss it out of hand.

A Buffer Zone

The United States formed military alliances with, signed agreements allowing the placement of American troops and other military assets in, and conducted joint military exercises with many of the countries neighboring China. The United States views these arrangements as agreements between sovereign nations, a way of burden sharing, and part of a drive to contain or "counter-balance" China; however, China perceives these moves as an attempt at Cold War-era encirclement. China has also sought military alliances of its own with neighboring countries, adding to tensions in the region.

These moves position American and Chinese military forces closer to each other, a proximity that could potentially lead to accidental clashes and conflicts. This risk has been highlighted by multiple incidents, including the April 2001 collision of a U.S. Navy surveillance aircraft with a People's Liberation Army Navy (PLAN) fighter jet over the South China Sea approximately 65 miles southeast of China's Hainan Island, and an encounter between a PLAN Jianghu III-class frigate and an American surveillance ship in the Yellow Sea near South Korea nine days earlier.[v]

Moreover, the various treaties and understandings between countries in East and Southeast Asia and either China or the United States have given several states in the region "a finger on the trigger" of a gun belonging to their superpower sponsor by stipulating that if the nation in question enters a war with one superpower, the other superpower will come to its aid. Some treaties explicitly entail such a commitment (e.g., the Treaty of Mutual Cooperation and Security between the United States and Japan, which is said to cover the Senkaku Islands). Others are ambiguous and easily misconstrued by the countries involved (e.g., the Mutual Defense Treaty between the United States and the Philippines and the relationship between China and North Korea).

It is therefore particularly troubling that some of these smaller states have engaged in provocative behavior. Such provocative behavior could not only lead to war between them and other states in the region but could also drag both superpowers into a confrontation with each other.

A grand bargain might include an agreement to treat states that share land borders with China similarly to the way Austria was treated during the Cold War: as a buffer zone. (One additional model is that of East Germany following reunification; a 1990 agreement between Germany and the USSR stipulated that although the former East Germany would be given the status of NATO territory, neither NATO troops nor nuclear weapons would be stationed in these parts.[vi]) Both powers would be free to continue engaging these countries economically by investing, trading, and providing foreign aid, to share information, and to promote educational programs. However, neither the United States nor China would be permitted to extend any new military commitments to countries in the buffer zone, and both would be required to gradually phase out existing military commitments. The grand bargain could also stipulate a limit to joint military exercises and the placement of military assets in this zone. Above all, both powers would make it clear to their allies that they should not assume the automatic, guaranteed involvement of the United States or China if they engage in armed conflict or war with either of these two powers.

Pathways

China is highly dependent on the import of raw materials and energy, a great deal of which reaches China via the sea. China sees itself as highly vulnerable because the United States, which has a strong naval presence in the region, could readily block these imports.[vii] Some American commentators openly discuss the option of such a blockade, which is considered a moderate way of confronting China relative to the Air–Sea Battle concept.[viii]

In response to these concerns and as a result of its broader interest in commercial expansion, China increased its naval presence in the South China Sea and developed a network of ports—termed the "string of pearls"—in the Indian and Pacific Oceans.[ix] Additionally, China attempted to reduce the country's reliance on shipping lanes by developing plans, including new Silk Roads, for transporting oil and gas resources by land.[x] Indeed, a system of roads, railways, and pipelines now extends across continental Asia.[xi]

Some Americans view these pathways as a sign of China's expansionist tendencies and interest in asserting global dominance.[xii] Meanwhile, some Chinese view American opposition to select pathways, for instance a pipeline from Iran to China, as attempts to contain China's rise.

The United States should assume—unless clear evidence is presented to the contrary—that extending land-based pathways for the flow of energy resources and raw materials will make China less inclined to build up its military, particularly the naval forces needed to secure ocean pathways—a win-win for both powers.

Responsibility to Protect, No Coercive Regime Changes

In 2005, 188 countries, including China and the United States, endorsed the responsibility to protect doctrine (R2P). Accordingly, the international community pledged "to use appropriate diplomatic, humanitarian and other means to protect populations" from genocide, war crimes, ethnic cleansing, and crimes against humanity if a state fails to meet its primary obligation to protect its own people.

However, in 2011, the UK, France, and the United States turned an armed humanitarian intervention aimed at preventing the large-scale killing of civilians in Libya into a coercive regime change. When the ongoing humanitarian crisis developed in Syria in 2011, Western powers openly called for not only ending the civil war but also forcing President Bashar al-Assad out of power. Russia, supported by China, strongly opposed these interventions. The two countries invoked the long-established Westphalian norm of sovereignty, which holds that no state should interfere by use of force in the internal affairs of another nation.

It follows that if the United States and its European allies limit their future armed humanitarian interventions only to instances of genocide and other crimes outlined in the original R2P resolution, eschewing intervention for the purposes of regime change, China (and Russia) might very well reactivate its support for R2P, benefitting all nations and peoples. Such self-imposed restraint on the conditions under which armed humanitarian interventions could proceed would further serve to defuse tensions and reduce grounds for conflict between the United States and China.

In conclusion

Several leading political scientists have argued that history shows that whenever a new power arises and the established super power does not make some accommodations with the rising power, war will ensue. This was indeed the case in 12 out of 16 such historical situations. Among the important exceptions was the way that the UK accommodated the rise of the US. To avoid the US becoming involved in a war with China, one notes that the two countries have many shared and complementary interests and very few truly divergent ones. Those could be settled, not by the US making unilateral concessions to China, but through a grand bargain. I have outlined some potential elements of such a bargain. It may well take other forms, however both sides have strong reasons to engage in it, and to counter the current drift toward war.

For more, see Amitai Etzioni's work on SSRN.

---

[i] Office of the Secretary of Defense, "Annual Report to Congress: Military and Security Developments Involving the People's Republic of China 2013," Department of Defense, 2013, Available at http://www.defense.gov/pubs/2013_china_report_final.pdf.

[ii] Miles Yu, "Inside China: Taiwan invasion exercise," *The Washington Times*, October 17, 2013, Available at http://www.washingtontimes.com/news/2013/oct/17/inside-china-taiwan-invasion-exercise/?page=all.

[iii] Harold Brown et al., *Chinese Military Power*, Report of an Independent Task Force, Council on Foreign Relations Maurice R. Greenberg Center for Geoeconomic Studies, p. 34.

[iv] "China, Russia and Other Countries Submit the Document of International Code of Conduct for Information Security to the United Nations," Ministry of Foreign Affairs of the People's Republic of China (September 13, 2011), http://www.fmprc.gov.cn/eng/wjdt/wshd/t858978.htm

[v] "China-U.S. Aircraft Collision Incident of April 2001: Assessments and Policy Implications," Congressional Research Service (October 2001).

[vi] Klaus Wiegrefe, "An Inside Look at the Reunification Negotiations," *Der Spiegel*, September 29, 2010.

[vii] Wen Han, "Hu Jintao Urges Breakthrough in 'Malacca Dilemma,'" *Wen Wei Po*, January 14, 2004; "China Builds Up Strategic Sea Lanes," *Washington Times*, January 17, 2005.

[viii] T.X. Hammes, "Sorry, AirSea Battle is No Strategy," *The National Interest*, August 7, 2013.

[ix] "China Builds Up Strategic Sea Lanes," *Washington Times*.

53

[x] "New Silk Roads," *The Economist*, April 8, 2010.
[xi] "Russia-China Oil Pipeline Opens," *BBC News*, January 1, 2011.
[xii] Ariel Cohen, "U.S. Interests and Central Asia Energy Security," The Heritage Foundation, November 15, 2006.

Mr. SALMON. Thank you.

I'm going to turn to Mr. Sherman and let him make his opening statement.

Mr. SHERMAN. And I don't know if there are other Democrats who would also like to make an opening statement. But none of them are indicating such.

Mr. Chairman, thank you for letting me defer my opening statement until after the witnesses. This is not our first hearing on the South China Sea. It's not going to be our last.

It's an issue that we should take seriously. But I think we need to lower the temperature. My fear is that we're making mountains out of reefs.

We should keep in mind that it is not just China, but four other countries that added dirt on top of various reefs in order to make them bigger than God ever intended them to be.

We should resist a tendency that I see at the Pentagon to try to reconfigure our military as one devoted to fighting China in the South China Sea.

I think that we need to focus on the threats to the United States, especially terrorism, also North Korea—the witnesses have mentioned Pakistan—and not focus on who owns the natural resources, which are not proven to be significant at all, knowing that the one thing we're certain of is that those resources do not belong to us. We should focus on the threats to the United States.

Now, we're told by those who try to hype the importance of these islands that $5 trillion of trade goes through the South China Sea.

That's true—almost all of it in and out of Chinese ports. The control of these islands—and I'm not saying China should control them—would give them the capacity to blockade their own ports. Not a major problem.

The second largest chunk of trade are oil tankers going to Japan, which may go through the South China Sea. Even if these islets were adjudicated to be a part of China, they could continue to go, and if they had to reroute themselves to go east rather than west to the Philippines, it might add a full penny to the cost of gasoline in Japan.

I would point out that while it is in the interest of those at the Pentagon that want to see huge new naval expenditures to tell us that these islets are of critical importance, they're not that important to the countries that claim them.

The Philippines wants to calm down. Japan is willing to spend only 1 percent of its GDP defending itself. They'd like more American tax dollars devoted to that effort.

And then those who exaggerate the importance, say oh, what's at stake here is all of freedom of navigation and maritime law, as if this is the only maritime dispute—as if China is the only country that won't let UNCLOS determine who controls what.

The fact is there are dozens and dozens of maritime disputes. The fact that there are maritime disputes, other than those involving China is rarely mentioned in this room because it has so little effect on the average American.

I would point out that I was just meeting with the Prime Minister and founding President of Timor-Leste. They want to go to UNCLOS to deal with their maritime dispute with Australia. Australia refuses, and yet we're not having hearings about how Australia poses a threat to the world and free navigation and everything America stands for, and I'm sure there's an Australian side to this issue as well.

But every other maritime dispute in the world not involving the United States is one we don't focus on.

Finally, I will respond to one of our witnesses who talked about not building missile defense in South Korea.

I would point out we don't need that missile defense in South Korea only if China defangs the North Korean nuclear program. I'm not sure they're willing to do that, and so to say we don't need it jumps the gun. We don't need it "if."

And one of the other witnesses talked about TPP. I think TPP is an incredible bonanza for China because of two provisions. You got to get down on the weeds on this. One is the rules of origin so that goods could be 60 percent made in China and 40 percent finished in, say, Vietnam gets duty-free access to the United States.

We get no access to the Chinese market under TPP, and that's if they admit, and you can be sure that if they admit that 60 percent was made in China the goods will actually be 80 or 90 percent made in China.

So this is 90 percent of the benefits of a free-trade agreement in the United States for China, 0 percent of our access to their market.

And second, the agreement enshrines the idea that free trade doesn't require that you give up currency manipulation. Those are two incredible victories for China, and they didn't even have to pay their diplomats to show up for the meetings. That's spectacularly good negotiating.

I yield back.

Mr. SALMON. Thank you.

I would like to ask the panellists, why should we care about the South China Sea? Is it the same as the disputes that Australia has or other disputes across the world when it comes to maritime space? Why is this one significant? Any panellists—Dr. Searight?

Ms. SEARIGHT. I will just say a few words. I'm sure others will chime in.

I would say that the reason why these disputes are significant is this is not about rocks and reefs. It's about rules and principles, and U.S. leadership in the region has long upheld a regional order based on international law, based on freedom of navigation, open commerce, an open inclusive system that all the countries in the region including China have benefited from, and countries in the region are looking to the United States to continue that leadership.

And so the anxiety in the region as China has launched into massive reclamation activities and built military infrastructure on those outposts—those artificial islands, which far outstrip anything—any other efforts that other claimants have done and other claimants, certainly, have engaged in reclamation and infrastructure development.

But China has done it on a massively different scale—over 3,000 acres in a very short period of time of artificial island building and all of the kind of coercive activities that have surrounded those efforts as well: Harassing fishermen, not letting Philippine fisherman, for example, in to fish in Scarborough Shoal vicinity, which has been their historic fishing grounds forever.

I mean, this has caused real anxiety in the region, and there is a strong demand signal—strong appetite for the United States to continue to step up and show support, not because we care ultimately over how those disputes are resolved.

If the Philippines does want to engage in talks with China, and they find a way to get to the table, I think the United States should support those efforts to find some sort of peaceful resolution.

But, you know, if countries want to capitalize on the legal victory that has really spelled out some of the obligations under UNCLOS, you know, I think the United States has a real obligation, certainly in order to maintain its leadership by continuing to stand with the rule of law.

Mr. SALMON. I just have a follow-up question, and I will go to you next, Mr. Colby. But my follow-up question is kind of an adjunct to what I just asked.

If the United States takes a back seat on this issue and we don't really weigh in on what's going on in the South China Sea with some of these disputes, what could be the outcome, and why should we care?

Mr. COLBY. Thanks very much, Mr. Chairman.

I mean, I think the legal issues are very important but fundamentally this is a strategic issue and what China appears to be pursuing or feeling its way toward with these salami-slicing tactics is ultimately military and political economic dominance, which will allow them not just to project power in the immediate area but beyond and not just in the immediate seas.

And I think the fundamental issue, sir, that you're alluding to is why would China stop and why would we expect them to stop.

If they're able to push forward and make a lot of progress and achieve power that they can use then why stop? I think we know, given their behavior, their ambitions which have expanded markedly, even in their own rhetoric and certainly their behavior in the last few years as well given their ideological system, their approach to domestic international order, it is going to be in a way that's unfriendly to the kind of order that we have built and sustained.

So, you know, just thinking about it rationally, if they're smart poker players, they're going to keep—they're going to keep raising if they're able to do so successfully.

And I think the other point, sir, that you're raising is right now is crucial because there are a whole lot of allies, partners and fence sitters and a lot of those allies, partners, and fence sitters and they're determining right now, okay, China is Asia's rising behemoth. Is it safe, is it prudent to affiliate with the United States to work to constrain and balance China's assertiveness? They're making decisions right now, and it is going to be a tough and continuing struggle.

If we are tepid and irresolute now, when we still have so many advantages, what does that say about the future? You have to say if you're a lot of those countries, I better make my case now because I don't want to stand naked before China, having alienated them.

Mr. SALMON. Dr. Etzioni.

Mr. ETZIONI. Thank you. This is very difficult.

I am surprised that the issue of freedom of navigation keeps coming up. As Congressman Sherman pointed out, why would China possibly want to prevent shipping from coming and going? I don't know they would survive 5 minutes.

I mean, if there is any nation in the world which is dependent on regular flow of raw material and energy from overseas, it is China.

I mean, nobody in their right mind thinks they would stop American ships and then Chinese ships would sail through.

So whatever nationality of people coming up, I think this question of freedom of navigation is really a difficult argument to follow, if you agree or disagree.

Second, as to the enormous military threats these islands will pose, they are basically like an aircraft carrier which lost its engines. They're marooned. Whatever two prop guns they have and one small Cessna, whatever, what are they going to do with it?

They pose no serious military there; and, if there ever was a war, they can't move so they would be eliminated in the first 5 minutes.

I mean, there can be all kind of reasons. As to the question that they violated the rules and, therefore, if we stand here they're going to overrun us everyplace.

As Congressman Sherman pointed out, if you allow the rules to be violated every Monday, Tuesday and Wednesday elsewhere and then we are now going to insist on them being protected in China, I am not sure that that will make us a very legitimate protector of rules.

The place to look at is not what's happening necessarily in Australia. The place to look at is what happened in the Arctic, where Russia grabbed a huge amount of territory and we looked the other way.

So yes, if you want to enforce the rules, yes, I very much agree with the previous witness. First of all, we should sign the rule ourself and second——

Mr. SALMON. Thanks.

Mr. Cheng.

Mr. CHENG. Sir, in response to this rule, I'd like to respond to this at three levels.

The first is the issue of military domination of the South China Sea. The Chinese were very clearly intent upon creating a strategic buffer throughout the South China Sea which would neutralize one of our key capabilities that we currently have, which is our undersea element.

The ability of the Chinese to create a massive network, which they openly write about of sonar surveillance systems with additional anti-submarine helicopters and the like from the various runways that they are building would pose a really serious jeopardy to the ability of American submarines to operate there.

Second of all, on the issue of FONOPs and why would the Chinese possibly cut their own throats, this goes to fundamentally larger issue, which is that China is, unlike Timor and Australia and et cetera, not simply focused on territorial sovereignty, but on the issue of rewriting the fundamental rules.

The Chinese treat their exclusive economic zone not as unique—about economic exploitation, but as an extension of territorial waters.

The same way we see with the East China Sea air defense identification zone, a demand that countries behave as though international airspace is actually Chinese territorial airspace where other nations must file flight plans and gain permission.

So, would the Chinese necessarily cut their own throat by demanding other people file ship movements, et cetera? That depends on how far we are willing to push that and how far we are willing to accept a fundamental rewriting of those international rules.

And finally, just very quickly, how would the region react? We see already that South Korea had to hem and haw an extensive amount of time before it chose to go ahead with THAAD because of Chinese pressure.

We see the Chinese pushing Vietnam very hard by declaring their oil rigs ''mobile national territory.'' That is a Chinese description, not mine, and have now apparently deployed military radars on their oil rigs.

So, the question that we have to ask is, how will the region react if we step away this one time? But, as my co-panellist has pointed out, the broader issue of what that presages and the implications of allowing China to rewrite not only the rules but to employ ever greater pressure.

Mr. SALMON. Thank you.

Mr. Sherman.

Mr. SHERMAN. Thank you.

I want to make sure that my views are clear. I am not saying we should step away. I am not saying these are unimportant.

But, when you compare these rocks to North Korea's nuclear program, to Pakistan—a state with over 100 nuclear weapons and a government is hard to view as a single unified entity—when we look at the threats of extremist Islamic terrorism, I would say these rocks are not among the top three threats to the United States and I didn't even mention the Iran nuclear program. First time we have had a hearing when I haven't mentioned the Iran nuclear program.

Mr. Colby, Mr. Cheng, you say that control of these island would be a terrible strategic danger to the United States if China got that.

But our position is we want this taken to UNCLOS which may very well award some of these islands to China, perhaps the very ones they need should the United States willingly accept any adjudication that puts China in control of islands when you regard the Chinese control of these islands as a strategic threat.

Or, do we bow to Dr. Searight when she says it is a matter of rules and principles, and if that means they have their foot on our neck by controlling these strategic islands, so be it if they won it fair and square in an adjudication? Can we—yes?

Mr. CHENG. I think that there is something of a difference between the person who walks into the 7-11 and pays $10 for a bottle of Mountain Dew and the person who walks in and takes the Mountain Dew.

Mr. SHERMAN. But the point you are saying is if this Mountain Dew is capable of being a huge strategic threat to the United States, then maybe it doesn't matter.

We are trying to separate here—I am trying to separate whether what's at issue here is the principle or the Mountain Dew, and you seem to say it is the principle—that if they get the Mountain Dew legitimately and they control these islands and they have the sonar equipment because UNCLOS said that some of these islands belong to them, that's fine. They paid $10 for the Mountain Dew. They get the Mountain Dew and they get the sonar, too.

I want to go on to Dr. Searight. You talk about rules and principles being at stake. Aren't they just as at stake when Russia occupies three Japanese-inhabited islands near Sakhalin? Aren't they just as at stake in the dispute between Oman and Yemen, the dispute between Iran and the UAE, France and the Comoros? Why is it that rules and principles are at stake only when we have a chance to confront China?

Ms. SEARIGHT. Of course rules and principles are at stake in all of those cases. But I think the reason why it is so salient here is because these disputes affect so many countries in the region. There are many claimant states——

Mr. SHERMAN. Well, excuse me. There are, like, four or five countries in these disputes.

Ms. SEARIGHT. Right.

Mr. SHERMAN. We've got a dispute between Madagascar, the Comoros and France. There's three. You can throw in Iran and the UAE and you're up to five.

Ms. SEARIGHT. Right. But then——

Mr. SHERMAN. So it is not like oh, principles are at stake when there are five countries involved——

Ms. SEARIGHT. There is——

Mr. SHERMAN [continuing]. In separate disputes but all with China but three countries that's not a principle.

Ms. SEARIGHT. There is—there is, you know, a community in southeast Asia, which there are four claimant states, and they have been dealing with China and with each other on these issues for a long time. And this is why——

Mr. SHERMAN. Let me finish.

Ms. SEARIGHT. Can I just——

Mr. SHERMAN. Let me—I've got limited time. Let me contrast this.

These islets have no proven economic value, compared to the dispute between East Timor and Australia that involves the Sunrise oil fields with $40 billion of potential oil and gas reserves.

Our principles are at stake. Should we deploy the U.S. Navy to force Australia to accept an UNCLOS decision? Is there a threat to the world because Australia doesn't accept UNCLOS?

Ms. SEARIGHT. This is why these disputes are so important. China has been rising dramatically as an economic power for a couple of decades. About a decade ago, it reached sort of an understanding with these countries that it would resolve these disputes peacefully.

It would put some of the real disputes on the shelf for a while. It signed a declaration of conduct in 2002 and off we go with China's further rise.

This is all about how the region, in partnership with the United States, can or cannot shape Chinese behavior. With China now going down a much more coercive track and seeking to intimidate, coerce, punish countries that don't give in to China——

Mr. SHERMAN. So the principle here then isn't maritime adjudication. The principle here is oppose China because—and you talk about rising powers. Over the last 10 years Russia has been rising. They occupy inhabited Japanese islands not to mention the maritime disputes.

Iran is a rising power. They have a conflict they refuse to adjudicate with the UAE. So, China is the only worthy adversary of our Pentagon, and it is perhaps just a coincidence that all these other things that seem to be in the same category don't merit our attention in much of the same way. I mean, we are not going to have hearings here on Timor-Leste's dispute with Australia.

I yield back.

Mr. SALMON. Thank you.

Mr. Rohrabacher.

Mr. ROHRABACHER. Mountain Dew, huh? Mountain Dew. I think I'd be more disturbed if they came in——

Mr. SALMON. Yesterday, it was Skittles, and today it is Mountain Dew.

Mr. ROHRABACHER. I would be much more disturbed if they were going into the 7-11 and taking beer, for example, and most importantly, if they were taking beer and were armed with a shotgun and had a bulletproof vest that might be of concern.

Yes, even more concerning than the value of the beer is that there is someone there with a shotgun, in your neighbourhood, with a bulletproof vest who feels perfectly comfortable to going into a store and using that shotgun to get what they want.

That's sort of what we are facing now, isn't it? The dynamics are changing in the South China Sea. This hearing is about whether or not we should be really concerned about it.

Mr. Sherman and I agree on many things in this committee, but I am very concerned about it. This is something that warrants concern.

The fact is that what we are talking about is there has been a massive increase in power in China over the last four decades and over the last four decades there hasn't been any liberalization of Chinese Government whatsoever.

If we think that liberalization means there would be less chance of confrontation of war, what we have then is a massive expanse of power, thus an increase in the chance of armed conflict and somebody coming in and stealing more than the beer or Mountain Dew.

Maybe, for example, the Vietnamese may understand this because a few years ago in this very area that we are talking about in the South China Sea, Vietnamese were massacred. Unarmed Vietnamese standing on some kind of a reef were just shot down by Chinese warships and so the Vietnamese haven't forgotten that.

Maybe some of us don't know about that. But the Vietnamese re-
member that, and they are scared to death of what's going on in
the South China Sea.

Now, so if the security dynamics are changing, I would agree
that that doesn't necessarily mean the United States has to be the
one to take up all the slack. We always take up the slack. We are
always the ones that have to jump out and pay the bill, send the
troops, drive our own country into bankruptcy.

Well, we can't do that anymore. That's another dynamic at play
in this world. I think it is time that we look, and realistically, at
the Chinese expansion of power in this society that's probably the
world's worst human rights abuser in the world in the sense of the
magnitude of it. So, how do we balance that off?

Let me just ask the panel very quickly. Doesn't it mean that we
should be thinking about working with Japan and rearming and
making Japan a more viable force in the area to counteract the
Chinese force that's improving?

Is that a plan, rather than trying to have the United States simply make up for it ourselves? Right down the panel, please.

Mr. COLBY. Sir, if I could comment. I agree with you completely,
and I actually think that the inequities of the burden sharing are
a real problem.

But, actually, I think the way to address it—first of all, because
China is so powerful, we do need to take the lead.

But, actually, that leadership role will be more likely to catalyse
that burden sharing because it is going to be so competitive with
the Chinese that the Japanese are going to need to, and they
should spend more. It's embarrassing they're only spending 1 percent on defense.

Mr. ROHRABACHER. You know, I would think of it more as a partnership with Japan.

Mr. COLBY. Yes.

Mr. ROHRABACHER. Japan is a modern——

Mr. COLBY. Yes.

Mr. ROHRABACHER [continuing]. Powerful country that we have
kept weak in their ability to influence international events like the
ones we are talking about. Now it is time to become a partner with
Japan and other countries in that region, but especially with
Japan.

Mr. Cheng?

Mr. CHENG. Sir, Japan, of course, has certain limitations, particularly on the nuclear side, that I am not sure we want to cross.

So while we would—I would agree with you that Japan needs to
play a larger role, we do need to recognize that there are limits but
that also means that there are other players in the region that can
also play a larger role—India, for example, which has a "Look
East" program, we now are allowed to sell arms to Vietnam.

We have limited our relationship with Thailand in the wake of
their coup, a policy that we did not do, for example, with regards
to Egypt. Perhaps we should reexamine whether or not we should
expand our relations with Thailand.

There are a number of other countries in the region that could
also be part of that burden-sharing effort. So while I absolutely
agree with you, I think we need to look beyond just Japan.

Mr. ROHRABACHER. Just to mention, I don't think that it would be necessary to have Japan or anyone else have nuclear weapons in order to increase the offset for Chinese strength in the non-nuclear area.

I think my time has run out, but do you want to have the other ones comment on that—the other witnesses? Maybe the other two witnesses would like to comment on maybe a rising partnership between India and Japan rather than the United States having to face it ourselves. Yes, sir.

Ms. SEARIGHT. Yes, I completely agree. I think India is going to be an increasingly important partner in the future. I would add Australia as well.

I think that the more that we do together with Japan, Australia and India not only does it, I think, send a very strong signal to China, but it sends a signal to the region as well.

You know, the region is very happy to see the like-minded large countries work together, especially when we include some of the smaller southeast Asian countries in terms of multilateral exercises or other kinds of things—joint capacity building efforts that we are starting to do with Japan and Australia with some southeast Asia countries like the Philippines. This is absolutely, I think, the way to go to network these aligned partnerships together.

Mr. ETZIONI. May I? I think joining Japan is about the most assured way to push all the possible buttons in China. If we are to really push them to mobilize and spend on arms, then we should do this with Japan.

I was born as a Jewish child in Nazi Germany, and I am following Germany. Germany really turned around. Never again. Japan hasn't yet admitted to all of the horrible things it did in China. So relying on Japan as a lead partner is highly provocative.

Next, every time we do one of those military alliances with a country in the region, we give them a finger on our trigger, and so we already extended a military treaty with Japan to those miserable islands. Any dispute about the islands now requires us to go to war, basically. So every time we involve one of these people.

As to the China military buildup, it built up from such a small base—you can talk percentages. They can increase 100 percentages, and they're still 100 miles from where we are.

It's symbolized by the fact that we have 11 aircraft carriers, and they have one. So I don't want to take more time. I know you know the answer. They are very far from the massive threatening.

Mr. ROHRABACHER. Admittedly, it started from a small base, but we have an expansion of power and, at the same moment, that doesn't strike me you have to worry about it. But, at the same moment, you happen to notice they are trying to make incredible territorial claims in areas.

Then they're going to say who gets to fly over large areas of the South China Sea, then there's something to be worried about.

Mr. SALMON. We need to move to Mr. Bera.

Mr. BERA. Great. Thank you, Mr. Chairman, and thank the witnesses.

I look at this slightly differently than my colleague, Mr. Sherman, in the sense that China is not following the rule of law and how we approach this is certainly important in today and the message that we send to the region about our relationship with the region—our commitment to the region.

But it also sets the stage for, you know, avoiding a kinetic conflict, you know, a decade from now or two decades from now.

Absolutely, Dr. Etzioni, we do hold military advantages far and away right now. But what we are doing is we are engaging in a region that is unsure of what the future looks like, that increasingly is unsure of what our commitment to the region looks like. You know, there's very much an interest in building commerce and trade and economic relationships.

Trade is a tool of diplomacy. Trade is about a lot more than the movement of goods and services. It's also an opportunity to reduce future tensions with China and bring China into the fold here.

So as opposed to always looking at this as an adversarial relationship—I mean, China certainly is probing us to see what we are doing and, you know, if we stick with that Mountain Dew analogy, if they go in and walk out without paying for that Mountain Dew today, tomorrow it might be a six-pack of Mountain Dew. They're testing to see what we will do and what our response will be.

That is why how we respond and stand up in a forceful way to the South China Sea. Yes, I am not worried that that is going to tip the balance of power today, but if we do nothing, well, they will take a next step.

And the reason why the South China Sea is so important: It is one of the most important throughways and seaways of goods that are moving in and out of Asia.

So making sure there's rule of law, that those seaways are open are not just important to us, but they're important to the countries in that region.

And right now, you know, with the fact that TPP looks pretty precarious, they're wondering what we are going to do with the South China Sea.

There is a real conversation going on in the region about what our commitment is. It's not all pessimistic.

I mean, the relationships that are building with India, you know, the fact that they are now our largest partner in naval exercises and the growing at least military-to-military, defense-to-defense partnership with India is a positive step.

The recommitment to the Philippines, to Vietnam, the opening up of these relationships are all positive steps. And it is not appropriate to say well, we are just focused on China. We are doing multiple things.

Clearly, North Korea is a real threat. Clearly, an unstable Pakistan is a real threat. Clearly, you know, tensions in the South China Sea are real threats.

What we want to avoid, though, is aircraft that are just flying around or ships that—you know, much of what you see happening in the Persian Gulf right now where you see provocative movements, one mistake leads to a war sometimes or leads to conflict. We want to avoid that.

I also think it is in China's interest. If we have this leverage, if we have economic leverage as well as military leverage, it does give us an opportunity to pull China into—to have a seat at the table and to talk about how we create this partnership.

They clearly are a major force in the 21st century. Let's try to figure out how we move this in a direction of mutual benefit and mutual partnership as opposed to adversarial relationships.

I guess, you know, the minute I have left if you'd like to talk about why this is important in addressing today in the context of avoiding that conflict a decade from now. Mr. Colby.

Mr. COLBY. Thank you very much, Congressman. I pretty much agree with everything you said.

So, just kind of building on that, I mean, I'd just say one—the one note of caution I'd sound is that I think our military advantages in the region are not as great as are sometimes supposed.

There's some very good unclassified analysis, for instance, by the RAND Corporation in their Scorecard report last year that showed that in a contingency over Taiwan or the South China Sea, if you just look out a couple years and the trend lines are not good—it could be very stressing for the United States and the nature of the conflict would be so difficult to control that it'll be a much larger thing.

And if you think our resolve is these are a bunch of rocks, the Chinese are aware of this, and that's why this perception now of trying to influence and show that we are going to stay.

And I think, addressing the ranking member's point, why it is so important to focus on this issue because China is the one country that could plausibly defeat us in a large conventional war if we don't play our cards right.

The Russians, if we don't play our cards right, could use nuclear weapons or the threat to terminate a conflict. But the others—you know, North Korea presents a very, very serious problem but the Chinese, if we don't play our cards right in the Western Pacific, we could be on the losing end and that will be a very, very different Asia.

So I think that's why we've got to front load resolve and show that we are committed and that we are focused, and then make the investments to maintain that high end. I think that is what the Pentagon is trying to do and I commend them for it.

Mr. SALMON. Mr. Chabot.

Mr. CHABOT. Thank you, Mr. Chairman, and I have to say it is been a very interesting hearing, so I commend you for bringing this quality panel here together. Really, it has been very interesting.

Mr. Cheng, let me begin with you, if I can. President Reagan famously had the goal of a 600-ship Navy. Does President Obama share that goal?

Mr. CHENG. Sir, I work for The Heritage Foundation, and I think it should be noted that President Obama generally doesn't really talk to us over at The Heritage Foundation.

That being said, I think that what we see right now is not a 600-ship Navy. There doesn't seem to be anything in the U.S. Navy shipbuilding plan to approach that number.

Now, admittedly, of course, we are under different circumstances than we were in the 1980s. That also being said, the kind of Navy we had with a 600-ship Navy was one that could support two simultaneous major regional contingencies.

It was one that could also fulfill a very robust strategic deterrent role. It was one that had ships such as the Spruance, the Oliver

Hazard Perry, the Ticonderoga, which operated 24/7 around the world.

When we look at how well or not well the LCS is operating, when we consider the fact that we now operate without an aircraft carrier in the Mediterranean on a regular basis. We do not have the Navy that we did then to fulfill the missions of requirements that we seem to still have.

Mr. CHABOT. Thank you. And it is my understanding I think we are down to, I am not on Armed Services, but we are down in the 250s, I believe, now as far as ships. And yes, some of them are more powerful than the ones when we—that we had when the great Ronald Reagan was President of this nation. But it is pretty scary, I think.

As a matter of fact, if I have my facts straight, I believe that for the last 25 years that China has increased its military expenditures over the previous years by double digits for the last 25 years whereas I think this President's stated goals has been to reduce substantially all the branches of the government. I think all the—not the branches of the government. I mean, I think much of the government other than the military should be dramatically reduced.

He seems to think one of those three branches is much more important than, historically, I think our founders envisioned a couple of the other branches.

But as far as the numbers, I think we are going to be down to numbers in our army that are pre-World War II. I think we have the smallest air force that we have had since we had an air force. Shipbuilding and number of ships is going in the wrong direction. So it is absolutely frightening, I think, particularly when you look at the world as it is today.

My colleague, Mr. Rohrabacher, was talking about has China come along. Have they liberalized when we have done things like given them most favored nation, when we trade with them all the time?

I think we have bent over backwards to have a cooperative relationship with them. Have they, just talking about a couple areas—maybe I've missed something—but have they changed their view toward Taiwan, for example, recently?

Mr. CHENG. No, sir. In fact, China has suspended all formal communications with Taiwan since the election of a DPP President.

Mr. CHABOT. All right. That's what I thought.

Mr. SALMON. I understand they also just cut the number of visas from Taiwan to China almost in half——

Mr. CHENG. I believe that's——

Mr. SALMON [continuing]. Just because of the election of President Tsai.

Mr. CHENG. Yes, sir. I believe that's the case.

Mr. SALMON. In retaliation or to——

Mr. CHABOT. Yes. Thank you, Mr. Chairman.

Have they moderated their views towards, say, the Falun Gong recently? Did I miss that, by any chance?

Mr. CHENG. No, sir. I believe Falun Gong is still considered a criminal organization in the context of the People's Republic of China.

Mr. CHABOT. Are they still rounding people up, putting them in hospitals, murdering them and selling their body parts?

Mr. CHENG. There are still reports to that effect, sir. Yes, sir.

Mr. CHABOT. I thought maybe they were still doing that.

How about the big aside, suddenly Free Tibet? Did I miss that one, by any chance? Have they changed their views toward Tibet?

Mr. CHENG. No, sir. I believe that, in fact, if you meet with the Dalai Lama, the Chinese Government still expresses extreme displeasure.

Mr. CHABOT. And how much effort have they made, really, to rein in, say, North Korea, which actually could be helpful to not only that region to—but world peace if they would actually do it? Have they done much of anything in that area?

Mr. CHENG. While they have announced sanctions and the like, there have been a number of open news reports about continuing Chinese trade, Chinese investment, Chinese companies continuing to operate.

There has been highlighted a case of U.S.-Chinese cooperation cracking down on a single Chinese company. But that has not affected, for example, the flow of oil or food into North Korea.

Mr. CHABOT. Thank you. Because that's something they really could do that would make a big difference to the whole world. I've long held the view that the only thing that will ever really get their attention is if South Korea and Japan—they don't have to have a nuclear program, but they ought to seriously think about one.

I think that would get China's attention and probably about the only thing that would get them to back down and to cooperate with respect to North Korea. I've only got a minute left.

I had a million questions, but let me turn to you if I can, Mr. Colby. You had mentioned the TPP—Trans-Pacific Partnership—and how if we don't move forward with it that it is going to send a message that the U.S. is otherwise engaged, although the public's view tends to be that that's just—that just helps China, you know, which is ironic because the reality is it is just the opposite.

If the U.S. doesn't with our allies establish the rules there then ultimately China will because they're the big partner in the neighbourhood and they bully everybody around.

But to be quite honest with you, both in the House here to some degree and certainly in the Senate, a lot of people are running for the high grass on that one. We've got both Presidential candidates—Hillary Clinton, who had said it was the gold standard, but when Bernie was chasing her around she went into the high grass too and switched completely, and Donald Trump, of course, has also come out strongly against it. So, do you see any hope there or what——

Mr. COLBY. Well, Congressman, I hate to—I don't know if this is good form, but I'd beg to ask you that question. I hope so. I mean, you know, I am certainly no economist and I don't, you know, accept appeals to authority on that basis.

But I did notice that I think the heads of the Council of Economic Advisors of the last, you know, six or seven administrations of both parties suggested it was good on trade grounds.

I am sure it is not perfect but no trade agreement, by definition, is going to be perfect, and I do know it demands a lot of sacrifice from countries like Japan that have resisted opening up for a long time.

And I think you put it exactly right, sir. If we don't set the terms of trade, this is essentially a gift to China, and I think Prime Minister Lee of Singapore and Prime Minister Abe of Japan and others have been quite frank in public, and I can only imagine in private, about what it will do to our position, but also to the kind of region that we want.

And, you know, when I am in Asia you often sort of get this idea oh, the Americans, are they going to be around? I point out, look, the United States, well before it got involved in Europe, opened up Japan in 1853 with the black ships and, you know, the open door policy of John Hay.

And this has been—this has been something that goes back to the beginning of the Republic 200 years ago. This is a core interest of the United States, and so no one should think that this is something new that we took on as part of post-World War II.

No, this is really core and, you know, I know foreign policy arguments don't necessarily trump pocketbook ones, but I think they should be balanced, and I hope that Congress will move forward on it.

Mr. CHABOT. Thank you very much. My time has expired, Mr. Chairman.

Mr. SALMON. Thank you.

We talked today about Mountain Dew and beer and all kinds of other things. I will use the Fram man commercial. He always used to say, "Pay me now or pay me a lot more later."

And I think that's the situation that we are in today. If we want to have a horrible problem, let's just ignore it because the more and more China bullies some of our partners in the region and we acquiesce or don't take part, the more position and ground that they gain it'll be very untenable maybe a few years from now.

And maybe the solutions then will either be impossible or incredibly painful as opposed to if well, if we act today and do what we need to to make sure that the rule of law is returned to that maritime space, then I believe that by doing that we actually avoid a much greater conflict that would be a lot more painful to the United States.

And so I really appreciate the witnesses that came today. It was a very, very informative session and my hope is that our leaders in this country keep a sharp eye on that problem because if it escalates it could escalate very quickly and very badly and the costs of dealing with a problem that escalates out of control are far worse than tackling it now when it is manageable.

So I thank the witnesses for being here today, and this subcommittee is now adjourned.

[Whereupon, at 3:15 p.m., the subcommittee was adjourned.]

A P P E N D I X

Material Submitted for the Record

SUBCOMMITTEE HEARING NOTICE
COMMITTEE ON FOREIGN AFFAIRS
U.S. HOUSE OF REPRESENTATIVES
WASHINGTON, DC 20515-6128

Subcommittee on Asia and the Pacific
Matt Salmon (R-AZ), Chairman

September 20, 2016

TO: MEMBERS OF THE COMMITTEE ON FOREIGN AFFAIRS

You are respectfully requested to attend an OPEN hearing of the Committee on Foreign Affairs, to be held by the Subcommittee on Asia and the Pacific in Room 2172 of the Rayburn House Office Building (and available live on the Committee website at http://www.ForeignAffairs.house.gov):

DATE: Thursday, September 22, 2016

TIME: 2:00 p.m.

SUBJECT: Diplomacy and Security in the South China Sea: After the Tribunal

WITNESSES: Mr. Elbridge Colby
Robert M. Gates Senior Fellow
Center for a New American Security

Mr. Dean Cheng
Senior Research Fellow
Asian Studies Center
The Heritage Foundation

Amy Searight, Ph.D.
Senior Adviser and Director
Southeast Asia Program
Center for Strategic and International Studies

Amitai Etzioni, Ph.D.
Professor of International Affairs
Director, Institute of Communitarian Policy Studies
The George Washington University

By Direction of the Chairman

The Committee on Foreign Affairs seeks to make its facilities accessible to persons with disabilities. If you are in need of special accommodations, please call 202/225-5021 at least four business days in advance of the event, whenever practicable. Questions with regard to special accommodations in general (including availability of Committee materials in alternative formats and assistive listening devices) may be directed to the Committee.

COMMITTEE ON FOREIGN AFFAIRS

MINUTES OF SUBCOMMITTEE ON _____ *Asia and the Pacific* _____ HEARING

Day __*Thursday*__ Date _____ *9/22/16* ___ Room _____ *2172* _____

Starting Time __*2:00pm*__ Ending Time __*3:15pm*__

Recesses ____ (___ to ___) (___ to ___) (___ to ___) (___ to ___) (___ to ___) (___ to ___)

Presiding Member(s)

Salmon

Check all of the following that apply:

Open Session ☑   Electronically Recorded (taped) ☐
Executive (closed) Session ☐   Stenographic Record ☐
Televised ☐

TITLE OF HEARING:

Diplomacy and Security in the South China Sea: After the Tribunal

SUBCOMMITTEE MEMBERS PRESENT:

Sherman, Bera, Meng, Lowenthal, Gabbard
Rohrabacher, Chabot, Perry, DesJarlais

NON-SUBCOMMITTEE MEMBERS PRESENT: *(Mark with an * if they are not members of full committee.)*

HEARING WITNESSES: Same as meeting notice attached? Yes ☑ No ☐
(If "no", please list below and include title, agency, department, or organization.)

STATEMENTS FOR THE RECORD: *(List any statements submitted for the record.)*

TIME SCHEDULED TO RECONVENE _____
or
TIME ADJOURNED __*3:15pm*__

Subcommittee Staff Associate

www.ingramcontent.com/pod-product-compliance
Lightning Source LLC
Chambersburg PA
CBHW081850280526
45789CB00007B/2634